Meditations o
Belonging to God:
A First Catechism

Peace to you –

Keith [signature]

1/06

Meditations on
Belonging to God:
A First Catechism

Keith M. Curran

Witherspoon Press
Louisville, Kentucky

Unless otherwise noted, quotations are from the New Revised Standard Version of the Bible, © 1989 by the Division of Christian Education of the National Council of the Churches of Christ in the United States of America. All rights reserved. Used by permission.

Scripture quotations marked *The Message* are copyright © 1993, 1994, 1995, 1996, 2000, 2001, 2002. Used by permission of NavPress Publishing Group. From Eugene H. Peterson, *The Message* (Colorado Springs: NavPress, 2002).

Quotations marked NIV are from *The Holy Bible, New International Version,* © 1973, 1978, 1984 by International Bible Society. Used by permission of Zondervan Publishing House. All rights reserved.

Quotations marked TEV are from *The Bible in Today's English Version,* © American Bible Society, 1966, 1971, 1976. Used by permission.

Edited by Rev. Dr. Martha Gilliss
Cover design by Rachael Sinclair
Book interior design by Jeanne Williams

First edition

Published by Witherspoon Press
Louisville, Kentucky

Web site address: www.pcusa.org/cmd

PRINTED IN THE UNITED STATES OF AMERICA
06 07 08 09 10 11 12 13 14 15 16 — 10 9 8 7 6 5 4 3 2 1

Library of Congress Cataloging-in-Publication Data

Curran, Keith M.
  Meditations on belonging to God : a first catechism / Keith M. Curran ; Martha Gilliss, editor.-- 1st ed.
    p. cm.
  Includes bibliographical references and index.
  ISBN 1-57153-023-1 (pbk. : alk. paper)
  1. Theology, Doctrinal--Popular works. I. Gilliss, Martha S. II. Title.
  BT77.C843 2005
  230--dc22
                              2005024837

*These pages are dedicated to the congregation I serve,
St. Andrew Presbyterian Church of Suffolk, Virginia, who
received them in sermon form with eager minds and open
hearts and allowed me thinking time to put the series
together. I am blessed to serve such a fine church.*

*These pages are also dedicated to my wife, Debbie, and
our four sons, Peter, Kiel, Todd, and Daniel.*

*I thank Sandra Albritton Moak at Congregational Ministries
Publishing, Presbyterian Church (U.S.A.), for being excited
about this project, and Martha Gilliss, Associate for
Curriculum Development for Adults, for her guidance
and help as editor and in getting things done right.*

Contents

Introduction

In preparing the sermons on which this book is based, I stretched far out on a limb and went against everything I was taught about preparing sermons. As a Macleod-era Princeton Seminary graduate, I know better. I was taught by one of the best preaching professors of that day. As a student with a preaching major and a worship minor, I was challenged by three years of his classes. Our senior preaching seminar for majors included a number of students who have become well-known in the Presbyterian Church, and I think I could have pointed them out back then as we sat around the table in the basement of Miller Chapel. I can imagine them following the Macleod method each week as they prepare powerful and Spirit-filled sermons. I confess that I have backslid and created my own method, for better or worse.

Professor Donald Macleod would have us select a text. (In the mid-1970s the lectionary was not a regular tool for Presbyterians but I am sure that if it were, he would have sent us there for our selection.) Then he would ask us to write down any first impressions prior to the formal textual study, in which we studied the text in the original language and used every commentary we could find. From that study and initial impressions, he would charge us to ruminate and pray for the Holy Spirit's inspiration to lead us to a theme statement or a purpose sentence. Once we could picture where the sermon was going and how it would conclude, we were required to construct an outline. Illustrations and connecting or contrasting Scripture texts were incorporated at this point. Then we were to write out the sermon in manuscript form. After a rewrite or two by Friday, we were set. Some chose to re-outline the message for presentation, while others preached directly from the manuscript. I continue to follow the latter style, and it has worked for me. The sermons included in this book are refined versions of the manuscripts I used on Sunday mornings.

The Macleodian format was *the* way of preparing and writing sermons for an entire generation of Princeton graduates, from the late 1940s to the late 1970s. But in some respects, I veered from the Macleodian method shortly after graduation and developed my own style. Although I incorporate many of the great techniques I learned at seminary, my starting place and stopping point are more Spirit-inspired. Typical starting places are a month or so of themed texts or a series on a matter of practical living, the Lord's Prayer, the Apostles' Creed, or the Great Ends of the Church. By selecting blocks of themes or a book of the Bible, I am able to plan my preaching themes sometimes as much as nine months in advance. This gives me a general direction. Each sermon is placed in a specific file, into which I am able to drop thoughts, illustrations, biblical texts, ideas from books read, and comments heard from persons, newscasts, or television shows. When I come to the file for the upcoming Sunday, it usually contains a handful of starter thoughts and some illustrations to use as building blocks.

I also have found that a theme sentence or purpose statement is helpful, but I do not use it as the goal of a sermon. Often, by the time I reach the conclusion, the theme I started with has been transformed, transitioned, or dropped as the sermon developed. So now I tend not to try to manage the conclusion before I start, but instead allow the Spirit to work—through the weekly process of study, research, text exploration, theme connections, and the rest—and lead to a more "natural" ending of the sermon. I am frequently surprised where it takes me. Sometimes I want to add a more fleshed-out conclusion than what I have on paper, but I have learned not to mess with it. This approach seems to work well for me.

I share this as a way to answer a question my editor wanted me to address. She asked if I would explain how I worked up sermons based on the contemporary catechism. Specifically, I started with each catechism question and answer and the corresponding texts that are listed after each question and answer. Instead of a three-or four-month block of themes, I had sixty Questions and Answers' worth of files with which to work. I collected illustrations and other material wherever possible and started to fill up the files. A month before the sermon was to be preached, I pulled the file and looked at it each week, jotting down some ideas and reflections on the theme and texts. Two weeks before it was to be preached, I did a more thorough study of the texts and topics, using commentaries and other resources from my library. The week of the sermon, an outline was set and the illustrations and background material were intertwined to form a rough sermon. Then I would type out the manuscript and refine it by Friday afternoon.

Because this was a theologically themed sermon series, I spent a lot more time than usual with the theology books on my shelf. I also found that I kept an eye out for denominational material on particular theological issues. The *Presbyterian Outlook Online* was a big help, as was the PC(USA) Web site. Making theology interesting for the congregation was another challenge. Although I have a few members who really enjoy a sermon that struggles with theological and philosophical matters, most people find that a bit boring. Linking text and theology and presenting it in a listener-friendly way required some creative use of illustrations and personal stories to create interest and to frame the more difficult concepts in ways that speak to a congregation as varied as the one I serve.

Prior to presenting the sermon series, I sent each family in the church a copy of the catechism along with a pastoral letter explaining its value as a faith statement. I encouraged families and individuals alike to use it in their devotional time and family prayers. New members who joined during the year and a half that it took to work through the catechism were also given the material so that they could feel included in the congregation-wide project. Often the children's sermon would highlight the week's Q/A theme as well. Occasionally the Q/A would be incorporated into the prayers in the service, and our music team based the hymns, service music, and anthems on the theme of the day. I did take a break from the series for Advent and Christmas, but picked it up again at the New Year. I planned to end with Question 60 and the word "Amen" on Easter Sunday. This allowed me to combine a few like-themed Q/As from time to time to fit the schedule.

The congregation received the series very well, and the printed sermons I provide each week usually ran out. I also received requests from missionaries, fellow ministers, and friends of the church to e-mail them the sermons each week. Knowing that the sermons had such value encouraged me to stick with it over the year and a half.

I hope these meditations will inspire others to realize that theology matters in the contemporary church. Whether they are used to supplement curriculum, or for personal or meeting devotions, or for general reading, I hope the Holy Spirit speaks to the church through this labor of love.

1
Who Am I?
John 1:12

W ho are we? Why are we here in the universe? What are we? The most basic yet profound questions arise from the simple wonder "Who am I in this world?" Science has tried to answer it. A recent educational television program stated that human beings are here on earth because a large asteroid crashed into the Gulf of Mexico 65 million years ago. The asteroid destroyed the dominant species of life on earth, the dinosaurs, and opened the way for the development of mammals, including primates. We humans would not be here if that six-mile-wide asteroid had not hit the earth long ago.

So . . . we are the result of a geological-astrophysical accident that happened sixty-five million years ago. That's one way to think about it. Philosophy has tried to answer the same basic question of life, but of all the volumes of philosophy ever written by brilliant thinkers from all corners of the world, none have come close to a satisfying answer.

Over the centuries the church has also wondered, who are we? Why are we here? What are we in the world? But instead of looking through a telescope or an electron microscope for a provable theory of existence, or mining the depths of the human intellect for a profound philosophy, the church has looked outside the created order for the ultimate answer. And only there has the truth been found.

In one era the church answered the question "Whose am I?" by saying, "I belong to God."[1] In another era the church wondered, "What are we all about? What's our purpose in life?" And the church answered, "Man's chief end is to glorify God, and to enjoy him forever."[2] In the mid-twentieth century the church asked the question "Why are we here?" The answer provided is that God created human beings so they could respond to God's love.[3] I was created so that I can return the love God shows to me.

But the most basic question of human existence has yet to be answered by the church: "Who am I?" Now twenty-first-century Presbyterians have an answer. A new statement of faith, called *Belonging to God: A First Catechism*, answers life's most basic question, "Who am I?"

"Hold it, Keith, a catechism? What's a catechism?" you may be thinking. A catechism is a statement of faith put in a question-and-answer format for easy learning. A catechism is a series of questions and answers on religious teachings. Our Presbyterian denomination has recently prepared a contemporary catechism called *Belonging to God* to help church members and their families understand what we believe. The time is right for such a tool.

Social scientists tell us that we are living in a post-Christian age, a time when our values and social norms no longer automatically reflect Judeo-Christian ethics and moral patterns. It is a time in history when pluralism and nonreligious values hold at least as much sway in society as the traditional Judeo-Christian value system, long the standard for Western civilization and the basis for our North American way of life. This means that much of what the church teaches in Sunday school, youth group, confirmation class, and in the weekly sermon is at odds with the values expressed on those endless repeats of *Friends* or the current issue of *People* magazine.

I remember being shocked one morning as I read in the newspaper that, according to a recent survey of prime-time television, the show with the most positive references to God and traditional Christian values was *The Simpsons*. Imagine that: the church's best hope out there in the vast wasteland of television is *The Simpsons!* We can use all the help we can get, but it is the church's responsibility to provide the tools to help us know what we believe.

Many of those who grew up in the Presbyterian Church in the 1940s and '50s ran recall memorizing the Westminster Shorter Catechism, or at least parts of it, sometime in their childhood. Ask a Presbyterian of the so-called Builder Generation, "What is the chief end of man?" and he or she will bark out, "Man's chief end is to glorify God, and to enjoy him forever."[4] The practice of memorizing the catechism has all but disappeared. Our denominational leaders have rightly discerned that now is the time to revisit the time-honored practice of learning the basics of the faith through the teaching tool of a contemporary catechism. The hope is that the newest generation of believers and their families will find the catechetical style of learning the truths of the Christian faith to be an exciting teaching method and a refreshing challenge for a new century. In a time when cultural values are often at odds with what we hear and experience at church, our denomination is offering an effective tool to teach our children, teenagers, and adults the historic truths about God as expressed in Reformed theology—in order to provide basic theological information to expose countercultural or New Age claims that disguise themselves as spiritual truths, to offer an assurance of grace and love that can't be shaken, to lead us to a saving knowledge of Jesus Christ, and to point us to our eternal home.

The sixty questions and answers that make up the new catechism, *Belonging to God*, are a great starting place for twenty-first-century Presbyterians who want to learn the basics of biblical truth and Reformed theology so that they will be able to express them in ways that make sense to our children, spouses, coworkers, or church school classes. In this contemporary catechism we find many of the answers people of faith are asking, including the primal question that nags at the psyche of all humanity: **Who am I?**

Three one-syllable words. Such a simple question, if answered truthfully, will offer the questioner a peace like no other peace on earth, a calm that no crystal sea has ever known, and a calling like none ever witnessed in the annals of time.

Who am I? Who am I in this heart-pumping, gene-packed life form?

Q. 1. Who are you?

A. 1. I am a child of God.

2

What Does It Mean to Be a Child of God?

Matthew 18:14; 1 Corinthians 3:23

The second question of the contemporary catechism is a natural follow-up to the first. It asks: "What does it mean to be a child of God?" Being a child of God does not mean we are childish in our faith. Being childish in matters of faith often leads to confusion in our beliefs. For example: A Presbyterian elder took along his young son when he went to the driving range on a Sunday morning. The little boy rattled his father when he asked, "Daddy, do you think God will tell Santa Claus we didn't go to church today?"

Childish faith does not produce proper perspective. But being a child of God does not mean we are childish. Biblically speaking, being a child of God is a way of saying we belong to God, our heavenly Father, our divine Parent, who loves us with a love that will not let us go. When Jesus spoke about the love God has for his people, he used the illustration of a shepherd who would leave ninety-nine sheep in the pen so he could search for one lost lamb. And the shepherd would not give up the search until the lamb was found and returned to the fold. As Jesus explained it: "In just the same way your Father in heaven does not want any of these little ones to be lost" (Matt. 18:14 TEV).

The Greek word for what we translate "does not want" is really a more forceful word than this. A better way to express the Good Shepherd's desire is to say that God has a "passionate determination" to hold on to every child of God. Being a child of God means that our divine Parent loves us with a love that *will not let us go*. There is a passionate determination on God's part to keep us in God's loving care.

Being a child of God also means that God is working behind the scenes, implanting a longing in our hearts that can only be satisfied by a personal relationship with our heavenly Father. Augustine affirmed that our hearts are restless until they find respite in God. As a loving Parent, God not only wants us to come into his presence; he also draws us in by that same parental love.

The church I serve has loads of young children. They run around on Sunday mornings in the narthex and really make themselves at home. To honor the importance of children in the church, the architect was asked to include a special way to recognize the children of the church in his design for our new building. He came up with a children's wall. Attractive bricks fill the wall in front of the main entrance to the sanctuary. On each brick a child is honored using a brass plaque with name and date of birth or baptism. The brick wall surrounds a stained glass window, created by a local artisan, that depicts the scene from Matthew 19:14, where Jesus said, "Let the children come to me." Children eager for a blessing surround Jesus. In the story, the disciples try to keep the children at bay so that their jumping up on his lap or tugging at his tunic with grimy hands will not disturb him. But Jesus orders his disciples aside and welcomes the little ones. They giggle at his deep Galilean voice and grab for his calloused carpenter's hands. And in his blessing of the children his voice is still reverberating around the globe two thousand years later. "Don't stop them! Let them come close to me. The spiritual treasures of heaven belong to children such as these" (Matt. 19:14, paraphr.). God is encouraging us to come close.

Biblically speaking, being a child of God means we are part of the family. The apostle Paul reminds us, "You belong to Christ . . ." (1 Cor. 3:23). You will never be traded to another team for a future draft choice. Your contract will not be bought out. You will never be laid off or let go or fired. You cannot be stolen in the middle of the night, locked out of your heavenly home, or cut off in a storm, because a child of God belongs to God.

Yet once in a while we forget that we are children of God. We forget that we have already answered the first question of the contemporary catechism. So it is important to be reminded of who we are. A classmate of mine at Princeton Seminary, Craig Barnes, has a great illustration in his book *Hustling God* about how we can forget that we belong to God. What would happen if a baby eagle were adopted by a family of snakes? As it grew up, its little wings would grow and the eagle would try them out, but the snakes would say, "No, no, no. Don't ever try that. Your wings are ugly. What you should do is crawl on your belly. Hide under a rock and bite anyone who scares you." Can you imagine anything more pathetic than an eagle pretending to be a snake?

Barnes says, "We can never justify acting like a snake just because we live in a world that is filled with snakes. Nor can we excuse our venom by saying, 'Just get used to it, because that's who I am.' "[5] Who am I? Am I a snake that looks like an eagle? That is not who you are! "You are God's creation, and he didn't make you angry, cynical, or deadly. You can pretend to be a snake if you insist, but God will never settle for it."[6]

Harry Potter lived in a muggle home. Muggles, according to the story, are non-magical folk. The family tried to raise Harry as a muggle. They did everything they could think of to make him as ordinary and unimaginative as they were. Harry lived a muggle's life that cramped his spirit even more than living in a tiny closet under the stairs cramped his dreams. Harry was like an eagle raised by snakes; his wings were tied. Then the letter from Hogwarts School of Wizarding and Witchcraft came, inviting him to attend the school in the fall. But the muggles would not let him see it. Hundreds of letters arrived, and then thousands of them that reminded Harry who he really was. Harry wasn't a muggle! Harry was magical! In fact, he was the most famous person in the wizarding world!

Isn't that what the Bible is trying to tell us? You are not a snake. You are not a muggle. You are not an accident of nature. You are a child of God. . . . Remember who you are and whose you are. It doesn't matter if you are white-collar or blue-collar, a Dead-head or a Parrot-head, a Ms., Mr., or Mrs. If you are a Gen-Xer or a Boomer, a Yankee or a good ol' boy, a Hokie, a Blue Devil, a Tiger or a Redskin fan, it makes no difference. You may be a Methodist or a Lutheran, a Presbyterian or a Catholic. You can be an introvert or an extrovert, a Democrat, Republican, or Green Party member. Paul says that none of these matter when it comes to who we are in God's sight (Gal. 3:28–29). You are a child of God and that means you belong to God, who loves you very much.

Q. 2. What does it mean to be a child of God?
A. 2. That I belong to God, who loves me.

3

What Makes You a Child of God?

Ephesians 2:8–10; Hebrews 4:16

G race makes us aware of the depths of God's love. As Martin Luther, the German reformer (1483–1546), once said, there is nothing you have ever done that can make God love you any less, and there is nothing you can do that will make God love you any more.

"For by grace you have been saved," said Paul of Tarsus (Eph. 2:8). God's love is unconditional. God does not say, "I'll love you if . . ." or "I'll love you when you do . . ." or "I'll love you under certain conditions." God's love is unconditional. Another way of saying this is to use the word *grace*. A crucial eccentricity of the Christian faith is the assertion that people are saved by grace. This is what really rattles our Jewish friends and baffles those who worship the God of Abraham in the Muslim religion. There is **nothing** you have to do. There is nothing **you** have to do! There is nothing you have to **do**.

The grace of God is something like this: God says, "Here is your life. You might never have been, but you *are,* because the party wouldn't have been complete without you. Here is the world. Beautiful and terrible things will happen. Don't be afraid. I am with you. Nothing can ever separate us. It's for you I created the universe. I love you. There's only one catch. Like any other gift, the gift of grace can be yours only if you'll reach out and take it."[7] Grace is a gift, and it is free for the taking. Some think they have to do something special to deserve it or work hard to earn it or be good enough for God to bless them with it. That is not how it works.

At a minister's conference at the Crystal Cathedral in California, a pastor told a story about an affluent woman who came to see him about the funeral plans for her husband. She said her husband requested two songs at this service, "Amazing Grace" and "I Did It My Way." We all laughed, but there are those in church who think that they not only have to be people of faith, but that they also must work hard to merit the grace of God. Our efforts to do it our way never total up to anything close to what God would require of us. When it comes to spiritual matters, we cannot have it both ways. The apostle Paul wrote to the fledgling church in Ephesus, saying, "It isn't by your own doing; it is a gift of God—not the results of your own effort" (Eph. 2:8–10, paraphr.). Grace comes. "Reach out and take it!"

All you have to do is reach out and take it. The contemporary catechism, *Belonging to God*, asks:

What makes you a child of God? (Q. 3)

The answer is simple and clear.

Grace—God's free gift of love that I do not deserve and cannot earn. (A. 3)

I think it was baseball manager Sparky Anderson who said, "Grace is getting something you don't deserve. Mercy is not getting what you do deserve." If that is the case, then he is a great theologian. God's love is both of these things happening in our lives at the same time. I hope they are happening in your life right now. In Hebrews 4:16 we find these words: "Let us therefore approach the throne of grace with boldness, so that we may receive mercy and find grace to help in time of need."

It is in this passage that we see how God's amazing love shows itself in grace. You can approach the throne of grace with boldness, expectation, and hope. It is what I call "unobstructed access" to the Lord of life. Confession, company, companionship, communication, comfort, courage, challenge, and celebration are all open to us because of grace. That is what we have now. Approaching the throne of grace is an important part of what will happen then, too.

Søren Kierkegaard, the famous Danish theologian, died in 1855. Although his books were complex and his disagreements with the church were bitter, his friends said that he passed away in peace and confidence, aware that God's grace was sufficient. This generous outpouring of God's love opened the way for him to approach the throne of grace. It will be the same grace that leads us home.

Yet maybe the more important focus for us today is how grace affects us in this life. When we are broken, the grace of God is the glue that mends human hearts and broken lives. Whatever mercy we receive in this life is a gift from the Almighty. Often it is what keeps things together when circumstances threaten to undo us. We may be suffering; nevertheless, Christ claims us as God's children and makes us whole. *Nevertheless.*

Listen to grace at work:

"I'm so sad to hear about Jack's death. Nevertheless, he was a believer and now he is with the Lord."

"I know it's cancer. It's going to be a struggle. Sure I'm worried, but nevertheless I can do all things through Christ, who strengthens me."

That little word "nevertheless" is a grace word. Use it often. It is like a bonus gift from God. It can help make the free gift of divine grace more real and tangible. Grace leads us to the throne of God and will lead us to our eternal home. And all this comes to us as a gift from God. Nevertheless.

Reach out and take it.

4
In Spite Of
Luke 15:21-24; John 8:7-11

Here is an interesting fact: You do not have to be good for God to love you! Whoa! What is that? You do not have to be good for God to love you. The fourth question of the contemporary catechism asks:

Q. 4. Don't you have to be good for God to love you?

The answer may surprise you. God loves you and me in spite of all we do wrong. In fact, that is exactly what the answer states:

A. 4. No. God loves me in spite of all I do wrong.

I was feeling guilty. The big-name speaker at the clergy conference I attended delivered one of the most powerful and stirring sermons I had heard in a long time. My heart was softened and my attitude humbled as I accepted the invitation to come to the chancel for the speaker to bless our ministries. I knelt down on the brown marble steps of the Crystal Cathedral in California along with hundreds of other men and women of God. But I came forward for a different reason. You see, a few months earlier I had had some fun at the speaker's expense. To make a point in a sermon I joked about the book the speaker had written. I didn't have anything against the speaker or his devotional book; I have even used one of his other books for a Bible study. But to make a point in my morning message, I poked fun at how an obscure Old Testament verse written almost three thousand years ago could generate a multimillion-dollar industry today. Now that speaker stood just a few feet from my bowed head, and he was praying for my ministry. I felt ashamed of myself. If I had had the nerve and he the time, I would have talked to him about it. But instead I just bowed my head and accepted his blessing. My heart broke. I wiped away a tear or two and walked back to my seat.

What happened that afternoon in a strange church? I acted out Question 4 of the contemporary catechism. "Don't I have to be good for God to love me?" I heard God say, "No, Keith. I love you in spite of all you do wrong. I love you so much that I sent this speaker, the one you made light of, to pray for you and build you up in my name." Wow! What a moment! I found out that the gospel of love is a lot bigger than any set of boundaries I can put on it; so big that God used a big-name preacher in California to teach a lesson to a no-name minister from Virginia. God really does love me in spite of all I do wrong! And God finds interesting and sometimes humbling ways to show me.

Two well-known Gospel stories tell virtually the same tale:

"Woman, where are they?" Jesus asked as he looked up from the dirt pavement. They were now alone. None of the finger-pointing men were around to see this part of the story. Maybe they realized that when you point at someone, one finger may be pointing at that person, but three are pointing back at you. He said, "No one is left to accuse you." He cradled her soft hand in his rough palms. His grip warmed her like a blanket straight from the dryer. Then he looked into her brown eyes, brushed back her hair from her cheek and whispered, "Neither do I. Go on your way. From now on, do not sin" (John 8:11 paraphr.).

Another time, a son had run out of money and hit bottom. The young man thought to himself, "How stupid I am! I can go home and work for my old man as a day laborer. At least they get paid at the end of their shift." Leaving the distant land, he headed home. When his father saw him coming, he ran to him and hugged him over and over again. The son began his prepared speech, but the father would not hear it. He took off his signet ring and slipped it onto his son's finger. At the party that night, the father said that his son was lost but now he is found, he was dead but now he is alive (Luke 15:11–32).

In both of these stories, a person was loved, even though he or she did not deserve it. Jesus loved the woman. The father loved the prodigal. Did they deserve it? Probably not. But that's not the point. What matters is that in spite of all they did wrong, God still loved them and found interesting ways to show them. Wow!

Curt Cloninger is a fantastic actor who uses his talent to teach about God. In one of his performances, he dramatically tells a story about a North Georgia chicken farmer named Raymond.

> Raymond drives a Chevy long-bed pickup. It is cherry. His mechanic, Bubba, says you can eat a fried egg off the engine—it's so clean. Everybody in town knows how Raymond takes care of his pickup. But in the cab of that truck is the most hairy, drooling, slobbering mutt you'd ever lay eyes on. Raymond calls him Partner. Everybody wonders why Raymond puts up with the hound who makes the front seat look and smell like a well-used kennel. The dog drools on him and sheds on his jacket and licks his face as he drives. When asked why he puts up with such a messy mutt, Raymond says, "Because God loves mutts."
>
> Raymond's chicken farm has over ten thousand chickens on it. One time, an animal was getting into the chicken houses and taking hens. Raymond figured he needed a watchdog to keep the varmint away from the chickens. His wife said that if he was going to get a dog, she was going to pick it out, so she went to the mall and came home with a French poodle. Now there is nothing wrong with a French poodle, but a French poodle for a watchdog on a chicken farm?

That night Raymond heard a commotion in one of the houses. He grabbed his shotgun. Without turning on the yard lights, he crept along the fence, and in the shadows saw an animal ripping at a chicken. He raised his gun and fired. He heard a yelp, and then that animal was long gone. He didn't have any more trouble with that varmint.

You may wonder, "Where was the watchdog?" Raymond said the poodle was asleep on the couch. It never stirred. That night Raymond decided he needed a real watchdog, a mutt, not one of those fancy dogs. Next time he was in town, he went to the pound and asked to see the dogs. The warden let him into the holding cages and Raymond looked around. In the first cage was the ugliest, hairiest dog he had ever seen. Raymond said, "I'll take him."

"You don't want him," said the warden. "Why don't you look at some of the other dogs?" Raymond looked around but then said, "No, I want him."

"No, you don't. He's no good. Take a look at the others."

"No, I want him."

"No, you don't. He's gonna be put down tomorrow. He's no good."

"No, I want him."

"No, you don't. He's full of buckshot. He's too far gone to fix up."

"Buckshot?"

"Yes, we found him along the roadside near your place a few nights ago."

Raymond reached in the cage and pulled the mangy dog close. He pulled back the dog's lips and there were still feathers stuck in his teeth. "That one right there is gonna be my dog," Raymond said, and he paid big bucks to spring the dog from the pound. Raymond paid even bigger bucks to get him patched up. Raymond cleaned up that dog. He forgave that dog and named him "Partner." And Partner has been his faithful watchdog ever since.

Curt Cloninger says there is a theology lesson in the story of Raymond and Partner. It is down-home simple theology.
1. God loves mutts and loves to forgive them.
2. It's better to admit you're a rascal mutt than to play like you're a pretty poodle.
3. Only forgiven mutts get to ride shotgun in the cab of God's pickup.[8]

The apostle Paul stated this theology in Romans 5. God loved us before we were lovable. God loves us in spite of what we have done wrong. But the message doesn't stop here, although this is really good news. There is something else that needs to happen. We are supposed to reflect this kind of love when we are followers of Christ. Yes, it can be hard at times to love someone else in spite of what they have done wrong, especially if the wrong was done to us. Try loving someone who has not yet come to love you. That is difficult, too. The love that is meant here is the love that we call kindness, respect, and compassion, not romantic love. We are supposed to show this kind of love even to those who really upset us.

The kind of love I am talking about here is love that deals with "stuck-in-it-itus," a common malady of humans. Stuck-in-it-itus manifests itself in irritability, short fuses, and a mountain of molehills. The common symptom is the repetition of questions beginning with "who," "what," and "why." Who is this person? What was I thinking? Why didn't I listen to my mother? Few situations stir panic like being stuck in a relationship. We may laugh at stuck-in-it-itus, but it is not funny when someone is in a situation where he or she feels stuck and has to struggle just to be kind and respectful to an unlovable partner, boss, neighbor, colleague, in-law, or fellow church member. Jesus himself knew the feeling. Consider the woman in John 8; consider the Prodigal Son and his older brother. From the cross Jesus saw those who put him there and he forgave them. At the Crystal Cathedral this author bowed his head for another to bless his ministry. Over and over again God teaches us humility: God continues to show that "No, you don't have to be good to be loved by God."

5

A Promise to Love

Jeremiah 24:7; Deuteronomy 6:4–6

So far we have discovered from the contemporary catechism that we are God's children, that God loves us, and that love is a free gift. We have learned that we don't have to be perfect for God to love us, either. Question 5 now asks: What are you going to do about it?

Q. 5. How do you thank God for this gift of love?

A. 5. I promise to love and trust God with all my heart.

What would you do if I called you and your friends a bunch of figs? A fig is a yellow fruit that, when dried and squashed, fits neatly inside a Newton cookie. If you are biblically astute, your initial reaction would be to ask if you are a good fig or a bad fig. It is better to be a good one, according to the Bible. The bad ones just get discarded.

At the time of the Babylonian captivity (sixth century B.C.), the prophet Jeremiah had a vision in which he was presented with two baskets of figs, one filled with good fruit and the other with rotten. God said the good figs were those faithful Israelites who had been taken into captivity. Those who had stayed behind and blended into the pagan culture were the spoiled figs. God said the good figs would come home again and would be God's children, who would love God with their whole heart (Jer. 24). Decades later, they did return and they did love the Lord according to the way God wills for all who are faithful.

How is that? With one's whole being. Deuteronomy puts it this way: "You shall love the Lord with all your heart, and with all your soul, and with all your might" (Deut. 6:5). You are to "love the Lord your God wholeheartedly, with your whole self, with all your capacity."[9]

God loves you! What are you going to do about it?

The catechism asks,

How do you thank God for this gift of love? (Q. 5)

We would do well to wonder how others answered that question. Theologians of the early church suggested that the love we need to show God is a blend of complementary aspects of our personality that together make up a person: mind, soul, and spirit. Today we hear that we are to love God with heart, soul, and strength. In like manner, Jewish scholars have suggested that we show love to God by offering ourselves to God with undivided loyalty, total commitment, sacrificial giving. Later, John Calvin echoed this interpretation. Modern theologians suggest that the command to love God with heart, soul, and strength suggests that God wants to receive back from us the totality of who we are as persons. God loves you! What are you going to do about it?

The catechism gives a wonderful answer:

A. 5. I promise to love and trust God with all my heart.

One of the best youth group games illustrates this answer quite effectively. The game has to be set up without the "volunteer" catching on. (In most youth group games a volunteer is also the victim of the joke.) First a volunteer is selected and asked to leave the room to read and meditate on a biblical verse about love. While the volunteer is out of the room, the youth leader tells the rest of the kids what she's going to do. She will blindfold the victim. (Blindfolding is another sure sign that the volunteer youth is going to be a victim.) The volunteer will be asked to lean back while keeping his legs locked so that he will fall backward like a log into the waiting arms of the youth leader. The youth leader loves the teen so much that no matter what happens she will not let him fall or get hurt. The youth director will say, "I love you and I will not forsake you, no matter what." But she will not say anything else. The rest of the youth group is to yell and cry out and scream warnings to the volunteer not to fall back because it is a trick and the youth leader has left the room.

You can imagine the chaos, as well as the volunteer's dilemma. Does the youth leader love him enough not to let him fall? Or should he question that promise and suspect that she has left the building? If you were the fourteen-year-old, what would you do?

Question 5 of the catechism asks: What are you going to do about it? How do you respond to God's love? We are to love God back with our whole being—with all our heart and soul and strength. But there's more. The catechism not only says we are to love God with our whole being; we are also to *trust* God wholeheartedly. The youth group game is all about trusting a promise of love. If we love, we can trust. Go ahead, fall backward—she'll catch you in her loving arms. That is the lesson we all need to hear, whether we are in ninth grade or in our nineties. If you love, you can trust the one you love with your heart and soul and strength.

I once heard a story in a sermon about a struggling young couple. There was a lot of month left after the paycheck was gone, and this put a strain on their marriage. The young husband decided to ask his boss for a raise. Before leaving for work, he kissed his wife, who was trying to steal an extra ten minutes of sleep. He whispered that he was going to ask for a raise today. She knew he was worried about their relationship and that he pinned his hopes on this raise. He had admitted that he was afraid that the trust she put in him on their wedding day would dissolve if he did not do something soon to better their situation.

Surprisingly, his boss agreed to the raise without question. The young man was a good worker and a valued employee. When he got home he thought he would surprise his wife with the news, but he saw that she had set the table with the wedding china, candles, and two tall wine glasses chilled and filled. Someone at the office must have tipped her off about the raise, he thought. He told her how it went, and when she brought in dessert, a note was under the dish. It read: *I knew you'd get the raise. You deserve it. The dinner is to show you how much I love you.*

After supper, he helped clear the table and saw a note fall from his wife's pocket. He picked it up and read it: *Don't worry about not getting the raise. You deserved it. The meal is to show you how much I love you.*

Total love. She trusted him no matter what. If you love, you can trust the one you love with all your heart.

There is a story about an old man who lay in his bed at home, dying. Under hospice care, he knew his time on earth was short. The family gathered and the pastor was there to pray. The old man told his pastor that at first he had a hard time thinking about his own death and that he could not figure out how to pray. Then a friend suggested that he imagine Jesus sitting in the chair next to his bed. That seemed to help. He would just talk to Jesus. He found comfort knowing Jesus was right there in the chair. Jesus was so close he could feel his love and the old man loved him right back.

The next day his daughter called the pastor to tell him that her father had died during the night. She told him that he had been resting and that she took the opportunity to do the dishes and some laundry. When she came back into his room, she found him dead, although she noticed a strange thing. His head was resting, not on his pillow, but on the empty chair that was beside the bed.[10] If you love, you can trust the one you love with all your soul.

Naturalists say that it is the struggle that allows butterflies to fly. When a caterpillar creates a cocoon, it is a new creation. At the church I serve, we demonstrate this miraculous change each Lent by bringing over forty creepy caterpillars into the atrium. We feed them and watch them form their gray cocoons. They are timed so that they break out in the days right before Easter Sunday. We fill a net full of butterflies, and we make a big production of their release following the service. It is a wonderful sight and the kids love it.

Right before the butterflies emerge from the papery cocoons, they shake violently, sometimes for hours. But the instructions say not to help them break out. It is easy to feel that we can help them and ease their journey to a new life. However, the struggle to break forth from the cocoon actually helps their wings develop and gain the strength needed to take to the air.

One time a cocoon fell from the netting and I picked it up in order to help the butterfly emerge more easily. That year, a couple of butterflies did not make it out of the net, and I could not help wonder if among them was one I had tried to help. You see, the struggle is what gives the butterfly the strength to fly.

It is because we love God that we trust God even when we find ourselves in the midst of a struggle. Do we love God enough to trust that the Lord is working through our struggles so that we may have the strength to fly, or in order to move us to higher levels of faith? Can we trust that God will listen to our prayers in a way that does not always give us the easy way out? Do we love God and trust God to know just the right measure of testing and refining needed so that we can emerge from our struggles strong enough to rise up on eagles' wings, to run and not grow tired, to walk and not faint? (See Isa. 40:27–31.) If we love, we can trust the one who loves us with all our strength.

Question 5 asks: Now that you know that God loves you, what are you going to do about it? And the faithful children of God answer: I promise to love and trust God with all my heart and soul and strength.

6

Two Postcards and Booker T. Washington

Deuteronomy 10:20; Genesis 1:28; 1 John 4:19-21

Two postcards, a poem, and Booker T. Washington can help us answer the sixth question of the contemporary catechism, *Belonging to God.*

Q. 6. How do you love God? How do we show, express, demonstrate, publicize, exhibit, carry out, and illustrate our love for God in earthly ways? If you have glanced at the Scripture texts that undergird this catechism question, it is easy to figure out. I will get right to the point.

A. 6. By worshiping God, by loving others, and by respecting what God has created.

By worshiping God . . .

The first answer may seem the simplest, but in fact, it may be a bit confusing to think about worship as a way to demonstrate your love for God. Sometimes worship is confusing. Take what happened to the little girl who sang a slightly modified version of the Gloria Patri one Sunday morning: "World with weird men. Amen. Amen," rather than the words, "World without end, amen. Amen." No one should confuse wonderful words of adoration and praise, the heart of worship, with the mundane. We should not be singing about "weird men," but lifting high the name of the Lord of life, Jesus Christ, our Savior.

At other times worship may seem uneventful, and it is easy to wonder if it is worth the effort on Sunday morning. We all would love to have an encounter with the Holy One but walk to our cars in the parking lot feeling let down. Wouldn't it be great if Sunday service could be as phenomenal as what happened to a Kansas City woman who went into an ice cream shop for a cone. After ordering she turned and stood face to face with actor Paul Newman, who was in town filming a movie. He smiled and said hello. Newman's famous blue eyes caused her knees to tremble. She managed to pay for her cone, then she left the shop, her heart beating a mile a minute. When she regained her composure, she realized she didn't have her ice cream cone. She started back to the shop and met Paul Newman at the door. "Are you looking for your cone?" he asked. She nodded because her voice had locked up. "You put it in your purse with your change," he said pointing at her pocketbook.

It would be great if once a week we could have a pulse-quickening encounter with an awe-inspiring person like Paul Newman! Yet isn't that what worship is all about? Jesus Christ, the Resurrected Lord, the Alpha and Omega, is here! He promised that when two or three congregate in his name, he is present in that gathering (Matt. 18:20). At the Lord's Table, Jesus' Spirit touches us in the holy meal, giving hungry souls satisfying nourishment. Maybe my knees should wobble as I stand at the Communion table and announce that surely the presence of the Lord is in this place! I wonder if we realize in whose presence we stand!

Q. 6. How do you love God?

A. 6. . . . by loving others . . .

In Christ we are challenged to live lives that count others more important than self. For most, this lesson takes a lifetime to learn.

I bought a postcard the other day while I was in California. It caught my attention while I was thinking about this meditation. It is a cute and colorful card with a quote by a youngster, age six, who puts the answer to Question 6 of the catechism as bluntly as possible: "If you love someone, hurry up and show it."

Consider Booker T. Washington. He was born a slave but was later freed. He became the head of Tuskegee Institute, a well-respected leader in education, and a champion of civil rights. As a boy, like other slaves in Virginia, he had in his wardrobe only one scratchy flax work shirt at a time, made of the cheapest material available. It caused pain just to wear the shirt, especially when it was new and stiff, but he had no choice. His older brother John would perform one of the most generous acts that one slave could do for another. When Booker was forced to wear a new flax shirt, his brother John agreed to put it on and wear it for several days until it was broken in—a simple act of brotherly love that was remembered well into adulthood.

Q. 6. How do you love God?

A. 6. . . . by respecting what God has created.

The fact is that there is enough to go around. God made the world this way. Yet sharing the abundant resources found in God's creation is a struggle even for the church. In the first months of the post-resurrection church, the believers shared their worldly goods and no one went hungry or homeless. But this is the last we hear of that first-century faith-based initiative. There have almost always been Christians who practice communal living, but for the most part, we Christians are locked into the consumer culture. I count myself in this, too. Recently, I moved my study across the hall to a smaller space. I was amazed at how much "stuff" I had accumulated in just three years. I packed up a box of books to give away and left a three-foot stack of books for our church librarian to look through. I filled a cardboard box with junk not even worth saving for the June yard sale. I know that in another three years I will be able to fill up another cardboard box. A lifestyle of accumulation may not be the best way of respecting what God has created.

On that same trip to California and in the same shop where I purchased the postcard that read, "If you love someone, hurry up and show it," another postcard caught my attention. Again, it seemed perfect for this meditation. This one quoted comedian Steven Wright, who has a line in his act that is custom-made for the contemporary church and for believers who tend to get caught up in our material world.

"You can't have everything. Where would you put it?"

Q. 6. How do you love God?

A. 6. By worshiping God, by loving others, and by respecting what God has created.

7

Seen and Unseen

Psalm 8:3–4, 19:1;

Genesis 1:1, 31; Acts 4:24

W hy do human beings make things? Why make a paper crane? Why did Picasso paint? Why were the pyramids built?

Is it fame or fortune that drives the creative force in our being? Or is it beauty? It is no doubt each of these things, but it is also probably more. There are millions or maybe billions of people who make things and never get paid for their products. Think of Emily Dickinson, who, once she finished a poem, placed it in her desk drawer. A farmer doesn't build a stone fence for the beauty of it. She needs to mark a boundary line, or keep the cows in, or just do something with the rocks she picks up from the field. But seen from atop a nearby mountain, stone fences appear like rustic sculptures across the landscape. It is a beautiful sight, which makes me wonder what the farmer was thinking as she patiently carried each of those rocks. Did she ever wonder if someone would consider her an artist, or even if anyone would even notice her work at all?

Is it just necessity that motivates human beings to create, or is there more to it than that? It seems that a basic human drive is to create. I remember hearing about the creator of the comic strip character Dennis the Menace. The artist explained how the idea for his comic strip emerged. One day he came home from work and his wife met him at the front door. "Your son is a menace!" she yelled. "You mean Dennis?" he asked. One of those idea lightbulbs turned on and a comic strip character was born. There appears to be something programmed into human beings that makes us want to build, make, and create.

Questions 7 and 8 of the contemporary catechism may help us figure this out.

Q. 7. What did God create?

Q. 8. What is special about human beings?

The answers to these two theological questions help us answer a more down-to-earth question, "Why do human beings love to create?" We create, we make, we build because we are created in the image of God. That's what makes us special. We design, write, paint, compose, choreograph, mold, bake, and build sand castles because we are created in the image of a God whose first impulse was to create all that is, seen and unseen. Our God is Creator.

Q. 7. What did God create?

A. 7. God created all that is, seen and unseen.

We can't help creating art, fiction, inventions, and new medicines because it is in our blood. Creating is in our God-imaged nature. Our God, in whose image we are made, is the Creator of all that is, seen and unseen. The post-resurrection church understood this well. In one of the first prayers prayed by the New Testament church, we hear, "Sovereign Lord, who made the heaven and the earth, the sea, and everything in them . . ." (Acts 4:24). The apostle Paul insisted that anyone, even if they never heard of Jesus or the Jews, can readily know God just by looking at the wonders of creation (Rom. 1:19–20).

At the Grand Canyon, a college student from Los Angeles was working as a tourist guide. One visitor asked him what had been the biggest change he had experienced in moving from central Los Angeles to the middle of all this. The guide replied, "In the city, you can look from horizon to horizon and see all that people have created. Here, I can look from horizon to horizon and see all that God created." The psalmist sang this Hebrew song: "The heavens are telling the glory of God, and the sky and stars proclaim God's creativeness" (Ps. 19:1, paraphr.).

In his book *Sources of Strength,* Jimmy Carter tells of an evening when he and his wife had dinner with the famous astronomer Carl Sagan. They dined at Vice President Mondale's home, where they enjoyed a slide show and lecture by Dr. Sagan. They walked across the yard to the Naval Observatory. While everyone took turns looking through the large telescope at the stars, Carter asked Sagan about current astronomical theories. Sagan explained that there are two theories about the universe. One is that the universe is expanding endlessly from a tiny point in time and space (singularity, or the Big Bang theory). Another viewpoint holds that depending upon the amount of dark matter in the heavens, the universe will expand further and then one day all matter will start to collapse and fall back on itself. Carter said the scientist denied believing in a Supreme Being and didn't want to talk—at least to him—about what alternative might exist for creation. Carter noted that according to the apostle Paul, such rejection of a Creator is foolish.[11]

Only when cancer gripped the great astronomer years later did Sagan seriously consider the power and source behind the mystery of the cosmos. In his novel, *Contact,* Sagan quite openly points to a Divine Being that holds the universe in its perfectly logical hands.[12] Thus, in our time we have the most eminent agnostic echoing the Hebrew poet of old: "The heavens are telling the glory of God, and the cosmos proclaims God's creativeness" (Ps. 19:1, paraphr.). The order and the vastness of the universe proclaim the power and majesty of a Creator who created all that is, seen and unseen.

At the speed of light, 186,000 miles per second, sunlight takes about eight minutes to reach the earth. The same light takes five more hours to reach the planet Pluto. After leaving our solar system, that same sunlight must travel four years and four months to reach the next star in our galaxy. That is forty trillion kilometers it must travel. The sun resides in the Milky Way galaxy, and the Milky Way galaxy is just one of a trillion galaxies in the cosmos. It is estimated that the universe is forty billion light years across and that there are about one hundred billion trillion stars. If you started driving across the universe at 55 miles per hour, it would take you just over twelve million years to travel one light year. And when you had done that, you would still have 39,999,999,999 light years to go. And the Almighty God created it all. Not bad for a day's work! "In the beginning when God created the heavens and the earth . . . And there was evening and there was morning, the first day" (Gen. 1:1a, 5b).

The perfection of the created order proclaims the glory of God, who created all that is, seen and unseen. Writing in the journal *Nature*, Benjamin Zuckerman, a professor of astronomy at UCLA, says that one factor contributing to Earth's ability to sustain life is the size of the largest planet in our solar system, Jupiter. It is a giant, gaseous planet with a mass that is 318 times greater than that of Earth, and thus it has a much greater gravitational force. It is this gravitational force that benefits planet Earth. When massive objects that could do great damage to our planet are hurled through the solar system, Jupiter acts as a sort of vacuum cleaner, sucking up comets and asteroids or causing them to veer away from Earth. Without Jupiter, says Zuckerman, Earth would be a sitting duck. The scientist says massive gaseous planets like Jupiter are very rare in the universe. Once again, we see God's design in creation. The proximity of a planet such as Jupiter may be quite uncommon, but it is no coincidence.[13]

Once again we hear an echoing across time and space. This time it is the voice of the Hebrew poet singing, "When I look at your heavens, the work of your artist's hands—the moon, planets, and stars that you have established and placed in their orbits—what are human beings that you, O Creator, are mindful of us flesh-and-blood people, and that you care for us?" (Ps. 8, paraphr.). The grace of God revealed in the cosmos proclaims the glory of our Creator God.

A professor was lecturing on the age of planet Earth and the relatively recent appearance of *Homo sapiens* in the ecology of nature. "If you were to telescope the entire history of the earth into just a calendar year," he explained, "humans wouldn't show up until just a few moments before midnight on New Year's Eve."

"Hey," a student wearing a fraternity sweatshirt shouted, "at least we made it in time for the party!"

It is not a party; it is an opportunity! An opportunity for God's highest creation to acknowledge the divine source of life and to bow in respect and awe to the Creator of all that is, seen and unseen. And it is up to us to take up the challenge of caring for the gifts God has left to our stewardship.

The title of Tony Campolo's powerful teaching video, *How to Rescue the Earth without Worshiping Nature*, suggests that some have gotten carried away with environmental activism. Yet this Christian professor believes that, despite the bad press, Christians are called to save God's creation.[14]

One day a commercial airline pilot decided that he had had enough. He had dumped his last load of jet fuel into the environment. The airline industry had a practice of dumping waste during takeoff or at high altitudes. The industry claimed that it caused no harm, but this pilot did not agree. He claimed that in peak seasons airliners dumped as much as five hundred gallons of fuel every day over his home near the Miami airport.

And so he celebrated his thirtieth anniversary as a pilot by following his conscience. He refused to take off until the waste fuel accumulated from the previous flight was pumped out of his jet. In subsequent flights he continued his demand, and two months later he was fired for insubordination. By now, however, his had become a *cause célèbre*, and other pilots rallied around him and refused to dump waste fuel. Finally the airline backed down and rehired the pilot at full pay. Soon the airline industry as a whole ceased the practice of dumping waste fuel.[15]

Living a lifestyle that honors God includes attending to God's call to us human beings—God's highest creation—to be stewards of all of creation. What you do in your life may seem small and unimportant in the grand scale of things measured in light years and galaxies, but as God's special creation, we have the ministry of good stewardship of all that God has created, seen and unseen. How awesome is that?

8
Imago Dei
Genesis 1:26–27;
Colossians 1:15; 2 Corinthians 4:4

The apple doesn't fall far from the tree. We are the children of our parents. We inherit many of their traits and participate in most of their cultural beliefs, even though as adolescents and young adults, we promise ourselves never to do such a thing. We even pledge that we will do a better job raising our children than our parents did. But the apple doesn't fall far from the tree.

A busy mother told a friend that she was putting a limit on her three children's outside activities. Her friend asked why. "The other day someone asked my three-year-old where she lived and she said, 'In my car seat.' " Our children are taking on our traits—good and bad alike—even as we speak. Sometimes our children share a lot in common with us, including our delights and our fears, and we do some things knowing that they are silly and unfounded. Even when we realize that our habits are silly, sometimes it is not worth the effort to change. So we give in, as illustrated by a classified ad that appeared on the preschool bulletin board at church:

For sale: Toddler bed, white metal frame, mattress, and sham.
Practically new, must sell, has monsters under it.

At other times we are quite realistic about those who are our offspring. A church nursery room had a needlepoint Bible verse on the wall: "We shall not all sleep, but we shall all be changed" (1 Cor. 15:51 KJV)—a very realistic understanding of the *nurseri-onic* nature of those who are created in our image. One of the first things God tells human beings is that we are created in the image of God, and God said that this is a good thing (Gen. 1). Ancient Hebrew patriarchs, Christian apostles, theologians from the Christian and Jewish traditions, and Bible scholars have struggled to understand what it means to be made in the image of God. Our contemporary catechism gives a standard answer, but the answer itself sparks another question.

Q. 8. What is special about human beings?
A. 8. God made us, male and female, in the image of God.

We get an answer, a very good one. However, we are then drawn to ask a follow-up question. We are created in God's image, but what does that make us? SPECIAL! Yet what's so special about human beings compared with a poplar tree or a quarter horse or butterfly? Theologians have come up with lots of great answers to the follow-up question, and most have their own unique contributions to the discussion of what makes human beings special in creation. If their interpretations were all true, we would have to build a warehouse-sized bookcase for the volumes of religious speculation about what it means to be created in the image of God. Almost all the creative answers that have come to us since Jesus' day have three things in common. To be created in the image of God means that human beings possess **a body, a soul, and a spirit.**

In the beginning, God declared that it was very good! Human beings possessed qualities that made them both individuals and spiritual creatures with the capacity to live in communities. But when sin entered the human condition, that initial image was shattered. The late minister of Tenth Presbyterian Church of Philadelphia, Donald Barnhouse, gave a good illustration about our shattered image and how it is restored. He said a human being is like a three-story house that has been bombed in wartime and severely damaged. The bomb has destroyed the top floor completely. The middle story has also been damaged, and the first story has cracks in the walls. The whole house has been doomed to fall down eventually but the family still lives in the first floor and occasionally ventures to the second story.

The top floor is the spirit, he explains. It has been destroyed by human sin. The middle story is the soul, damaged and of little use. The first floor is the body, cracked and doomed to die. Fortunately for us God's Son is a carpenter and a very good one. He is the best. And Jesus goes to work on this old house, starting with the top floor. He makes a brand new spirit for us so that we experience rebirth or salvation. Then he repairs the middle story and remodels it into his own image. This is the work of sanctification, or spiritual maturation. And finally he takes care of the first floor. At the resurrection when Christ returns, the body will be transformed into a spiritual form for eternal living.[16]

In this metaphor, Barnhouse illustrates how the restorative work of Jesus Christ encompasses the whole person as we are restored to the image of God, which is now fully seen only in Jesus Christ, God's Son. When we look at Jesus, we see what God had in mind when he created humanity in God's own image—a creature possessing a body, soul, and spirit. This is what makes human beings special in the created order. We are created, male and female, in God's image.

   a. *Body.* When theologians talk about the body, they are referring to that which makes us individual human beings. We possess personality, something that God also possesses but plants and rocks do not. Personality involves the possession of physical life as well as of knowledge, feelings (including religious feelings, in the case of God and humans), creativity, imagination, and will. God has personality, and so do we.

It is only partially true to say that a pet has personality, or that a plant can sense emotion. As a quality of being designed in the image of God, personality links humanity with God in a unique and God-designed way. And when we wonder whether God has a body after which our human frame is modeled, we have to remember that God came to human beings in physical form—in Jesus of Nazareth, a flesh-and-blood person. But God also walked in the garden with Adam and Eve, wrestled with Jacob, spoke to Moses, and soared through the air in the form of a dove. It is not too far-fetched to think that God showed up in bodily form from time to time. God is a living God and shares all the qualities that make us human. That makes us special!

Our bodies are of great value and we are to treat them with honor and respect. Not only are our bodies created according to God's design, but our lives also have been redeemed by Christ. It is important always to understand that the human body is God's temple, a dwelling place for the Spirit of God (1 Cor. 6:19).

    b. *Soul.* Theologian James Boice says that it may well be that the soul centers in the mind, and that it includes all likes and dislikes, special talents and giftedness, weaknesses, emotions, aspirations, and anything else that distinguishes us from all others of our species. Because we have souls, we can have relationships with others and live in community.[17] God created humans to be in a loving relationship with our Creator. To be made in the image of God means we share the ability to build relationships based on love and life in community. Refusal to love our sister or brother is a denial of one's own God-imaged nature. That we have a soul means that we all belong to Christ's community on our day of baptism.

The apostle John advised the post-resurrection church to build a community based on love. Hate, prejudice, abusive relationships, manipulation of power, and misuse of wealth are denials that we are created in the image of God. Having a soul means that we possess a moral sense as well as a personality. It means that God created us with two things that characterize God's life: freedom and responsibility.

Adam and Eve were not automatons; rather, they were free to make decisions and to be responsible for their actions. Yet since the Fall, humanity's freedom has been limited. As Augustine of Hippo put it: Before the Fall Adam and Eve were able not to sin, but after the Fall they were not able not to sin. This limited freedom causes much pain, inasmuch as it cannot be loosed from our sinful nature. We are free, but not free not to sin.

A cigar smoker bought several hundred designer cigars valued at $15,000 and then had them insured against fire. After he smoked them all, he filed a claim saying that the cigars been destroyed by fire. The insurance company refused to pay, and the man sued. A judge ruled that because the insurance company had in fact agreed to insure the cigars against fire, it was legally responsible. The company had no choice but to pay the claim. Then, when the man accepted the money, the insurance company had him arrested for arson. It seems we are not able not to sin and we end up paying the price.

Our freedom and responsibility are qualities shared with the Creator of the universe, yet the freedom we experience is restricted by the human condition.

We are taught to think that we are free (2 Cor. 4:4), but in reality we need Jesus to set us free from the grip of a distorted and limited earthly reality where we are not able not to sin.

    c. *Spirit.* Those created in God's image have a spirit. We possess personality, morality, and spirituality. Humanity exists for communication with God.[18] We have physical bodies, just as animals and plants do. We have souls, which bring us into community with others of our species and our natural surroundings. But it is the spirit that makes us more special. It is on the level of spirituality that we are aware of God and have a desire to interact with the Creator, who is Spirit (John 4:24).

Without the proverbial third floor built by carpenter Jesus, people long for a connection with God but cannot find it. The stairs upward lead nowhere. We hide from God but claim that God is impossible to find. David Bailey, a Christian singer and songwriter, skillfully expresses the struggle and longing to connect with the Spirit of God. In his song "Trying to Believe" he takes us along on the quest of a human body and soul to find one's spirit:

    I don't know where this road is going . . . I'm just trying to believe . . .

    I don't know who's doing the talking, got so many voices in my head . . .

    Every time [I] take a right turn, seems I should have taken a left instead . . .

    I don't know when I'll find the answers; I'm just trying to believe;

    I've got dozens of doubts on my doorstep . . . I've just now started trying to believe in you.[19]

But when Jesus builds a new spirit with his own hands, when we are born again in Christ, we start to hear a gentle voice coming from the third floor: "Seek me, and you shall live" (Amos 5:4, paraphr.). It is then that our spirit is crafted by the skillful hands of the Carpenter and we find a connection to God.

Maybe you are just beginning to discover that the Carpenter from Nazareth is building a new third floor in your life. Or perhaps you have not ventured up the stairs for quite some time. This prayer may be especially appropriate for you today:

    Sometimes, God, you are not very easy to see. Maybe that's because I am being half-hearted about looking. Help me find my way to the third floor of my spiritual home. Remind me to live on all three levels so that my whole life will reflect your image, my Lord and Creator. Help me to remember that you are not far from any of us. In fact, you are very close to each of us now. We each know that and we believe it. Amen.

9

Living in the Image of God

Matthew 5:14-16; 2 Corinthians 4:5-6

Q. 9. What does it mean that we are made in God's image?
A. 9. It means we are made to reflect God's goodness, wisdom, and love.

The answer is more a reflection of what God intends than a present reality. As when a parent hopes that a daughter or son will grow up to be like mom or dad, the result is often disappointing.

I remember a story about a physician dropping off her four-year-old daughter at preschool. On the way there, the doctor noticed that her daughter had picked up her stethoscope from the front seat of the car and was playing with it. The child put the earpieces in her ears and was listening intently. "Be still, my heart," her mother said to herself. "My little girl wants to follow in mommy's footsteps and be a doctor! Alleluia!" Then she heard her precious little angel speak into the round end: "Welcome to Burger King. May I take your order?"

Sometimes we do not reflect our parents' high hopes and dreams for us. I wonder if God, our heavenly parent, ever thinks that way about us. As God's special creation, each of us with a body, soul, and spirit made in the image of God, we are to reflect God's high hopes and dreams for us. According to the contemporary catechism, these hopes and dreams include our desire to reflect God's goodness, wisdom, and love. That is what God intends for creation.

To reflect God's goodness

I am impressed with a Bible verse I found hidden among the theological arguments in Paul's letter to the Romans. I have shared that discovery with my students in Bible study as well as with people who stopped by. I have added the verse to pastoral notes I sent out and even quoted it to my wife's boss when we visited him in the hospital. It is one of those unique treasures hidden among the ink and paper and footnotes of a Bible that one comes across every so often. It made me shout, "Holy cow! What a find!"

It was providential, too. I found it during the very week I could use it in the sermon based on Question 9 of the catechism. I think it is an example of the goodness of God, the goodness that we are challenged to reflect in our own spiritual lives. The verse refers to Abraham, the father of three world religions: Judaism, Christianity, and Islam. It is a complement to his faith in God's goodness. The verse is a good one to memorize or write on a Post-it and stick on your desk or the dashboard of your car. Are you ready for it? Well, here it is. Romans 4:21 says of Abraham: "He was absolutely sure that God would be able to do what he had promised" (TEV).

This meant that God gave him a homeland, a child in his old age, a ram in the bush, and descendants numerous enough to become many nations. Abraham observed, again and again, the goodness of God in his life. Again and again God's hand gently and at times forcefully directed him, rescued him, guided him, slowed him down, and stopped him on his journey. Providence, mercy, grace, forgiveness, protection, and steadfast love came his way from the Lord, and with each installment Abraham's appreciation of the goodness of God grew.

Jesus instructed two of his disciples to find him a donkey. It was Passover and he was ready to raise people's awareness of his mission by making a dramatic entry into the holy city of Jerusalem. He told two of them where and how to secure a young donkey for him to ride. Everything went as planned. It is likely the two disciples on their return trip said something like, "We're absolutely sure that Jesus can do what he has promised."

"God is good . . . all the time! All the time . . . God is good!" This is the standard credo of those who do an Emmaus Walk, a kind of Presbyterian pilgrimage. This energetic creed must be based on Romans 4:21: "We are absolutely sure that God is able to do what God has promised" (paraphr.). This is the goodness we are asked to reflect in our little corner of the world. Show your faith and keep your promises. Make your word your bond. Tell the truth. Be trustworthy. Let your yes be yes and your no be no. Wouldn't it be great to hear others say about you that they can count on you no matter what? Reflect God's goodness by trusting God's promises and keeping your own.

To reflect God's wisdom

An angel appears at a faculty meeting and tells the dean that in return for his unselfish acts of kindness at the college, the Lord will reward him with his choice of unlimited wealth, wisdom, or beauty. Without hesitating, the scholar selects wisdom. "Done!" says the angel, and he disappears in a puff of smoke. Now, all heads turn toward the dean, waiting for his first words of wisdom. Nothing comes. Someone says, "Say something wise." The dean looks at them and, shaking his head, says, "I should have taken the money."

Wisdom came too late for him. It is not too late for us. The wisdom we are to reflect is the wisdom we see in God's relationship with us and the world. The Talmud, a Jewish collection of teachings, records that kindness is the highest wisdom. Having the wisdom to be kind often keeps one out of trouble. A newspaper columnist noted that intelligence is spotting the flaw in your boss's reasoning. Wisdom is refraining from pointing it out.

God-inspired wisdom comes at a cost. When we are in pain we tend to try to figure out why, and we become wiser as a result and learn better ways to navigate life. It is a good thing when we mature to the point at which we can understand that having an opinion does not make us right. Reinhold Niebuhr wrote what has come to be known as the Serenity Prayer: "God grant me the serenity to accept the things I cannot change, the courage to change the things I can, and the wisdom to know the difference."

The wisdom we reflect is not perfect. Perfection is reserved only for the Creator. But it is possible for us to be mirrors of this wisdom. A mirror reflects a two-dimensional image of a three-dimensional reality. Our wisdom, though not perfect, is a start. It still needs constant reality checks and is filled with compromise. Human wisdom always requires humility in order that it may reflect something similar to God's perfect wisdom. But it is a start. Being made in God's image means we reflect the goodness and the wisdom of God.

To reflect God's love

The story of Jesus' triumphal entry into Jerusalem offers insight into three expressions of love: radiant love, servant love, tough love.

My wife has a little two- by three-inch picture in a plastic frame of her favorite picture of Jesus. It is the Laughing Jesus. His head is thrown back, his hands on his belly, and he is laughing with such gusto that it is hard not to smile when you see it. It is easy for me to picture Jesus laughing like that as he rode up the dusty path on the back of a little gray donkey to the gates of Jerusalem. This is radiant love. It is a love that comes with a prescription: SMILE. Love that radiates from the heart and erupts into laughter and joy is the love God desires from us. It is that old bumper sticker from the '70s: "Smile, God Loves You!"

There is another kind of love: servant love. This is love that begins with a choice. A little more than one hundred and fifty years before Jesus rode into Jerusalem to songs and shouts of praise and hosannas, another man the people called "messiah" traveled up the same dusty path to shouts of "Hosanna!" and "Blessed is he who comes in the name of the Lord!" Palms waved, linen shirts turned into impromptu flags, and children ran beside the procession, waving arms and hollering at the top of their lungs. But this "hero" chose to ride a stallion, a war steed. He chose to be identified with the symbol of conquering warrior king. His name was Judas Maccabeus, the Jewish general who won independence for Israel from the Syrians in 168 B.C. Now over a century and a half later, another hero rides up the dusty path to the holy city of Jerusalem to shouts of "Hosanna! Blessed is the one who comes in the name of the Lord," but this man chooses to ride a gray beast of burden, the symbol of a humble servant. He chooses to be identified with servanthood. Jesus' triumphal entry shows us another expression of love; servant love. It is based on a choice, a choice to count others more important than oneself. It is a choice to serve the one who entered riding a donkey instead of the one who mounted a steed. It is a choice made by his followers to serve him by serving others in his name. It is a choice God wants each of us to make daily.

Servant love is risky and unpredictable. Oftentimes, we may not even know if we are doing it right. Simple acts of kindness—a sympathetic touch on the shoulder, a visit to a sick friend, or a smile when words refuse to come—are all possible expressions of servant love. Today, more than ever, God's people need to make the choice to love others by showing kindness and mercy to everyone, everywhere, every day. As a pastor said at a caregivers conference, "Ninety percent of helping is just showing up!" Choose to show up and you will be reflecting the love Jesus loved to show: servant love.

A third expression of love is seen in the Palm Sunday story at the end of Jesus' ride into Jerusalem. What he saw made his blood boil. The holiday pilgrims huddled around dozens of kiosks, changing their secular coins into temple currency. Dickering for a lamb, bartering for a turtledove, the cacophony of bargain hunters dealing for the best price drowned out the chanting psalms of worshipers. The scene drew tough love from the Savior. Over the tables turned! "My house will be a house of prayer—not a den of thieves."

There are times when love must be tough. Occasionally even advocates of nonviolence recognize that some circumstances cannot adequately be addressed by gentle approaches to achieving peace. Conventional care and kindness may not be enough. Tough love, for instance, has to be shown to those whose conduct is reckless or puts others in danger. Tough love has to be shown to those who threaten disharmony in a household, workplace, or house of worship. Strict rules, zero tolerance for repeated bad behavior or misconduct may seem merciless, but sometimes sweetness, patience, and fourth or fifth chances do little to improve a situation. Tough love will. It is not a prescription for every situation or family crisis, but sometimes nothing less will work. The account of Jesus' triumphal entry into Jerusalem can help us realize that sometimes the love we offer may have to show itself in stoutness, other times in servanthood, and quite often with a radiant expression of joy accented by laughter.

Those created in the image of God reflect the goodness, wisdom, and love modeled for the world in the life, death, and resurrection of Jesus of Nazareth.

10

Why Then . . . ?

Genesis 4:8; Romans 7:19-20

I laughed when I read a cute e-mail forwarded to me from a church member who reported that, at a women's Bible study group one night, the women were speculating on how many apples Adam and Eve ate in the Garden of Eden. The friendly banter turned into an argument when one of the newer members declared, "One, of course!"

A woman who had been around a bit longer corrected her. "No, my dear. Eve 8 and Adam did 2. That makes 10."

"No," one of the older women said. "You two are new so maybe you don't know that Eve 8 and Adam 8 also. That makes 16."

Joining the discussion, the president of the women's group explained with authority, "No, Eve 8-1 and Adam 8-1-2. Add that up and it's 893."

The pastor's wife got into the discussion. "I'm sorry to disagree but I've been around church a long time and I know that Eve 8-1-4 Adam and Adam 8-1-2-4 Eve. That would bring the total to 8,938."

Luckily, before any fists started to fly, the sexton came into the room and, hearing the argument, announced that they were all wrong. "It's 0. The Bible says they ate no apples. Check it out yourself."

They did and sure enough, the sexton was right. Nowhere in the creation story does it say anything about an "apple."

The theological theme of their argument is original sin, and the contemporary catechism, *Belonging to God,* can help us discover what Christians believe about sin in the world. The next few questions deal with sin.

Q. 10. Why, then, do we human beings often act in destructive and hateful ways?

A. 10. Because we have turned away from God and fallen into sin.

Someone said that the trouble with trouble is that it usually starts out as a whole lot of fun. A young man asked for his share of his father's estate, cashed it out, packed a bag, and headed for a faraway country. There he spent the entire roll of bills on fast women, fast cars, and fast food. When it was gone, he hit rock bottom—no job, no money, no friends, no dignity, and no options, except one: home. Ashamed, he started home with his last ounce of strength in hopes of at least working as a day laborer on his father's farm. At least he could earn enough to get some hot food and a place to stay. What had started out as loads of fun shortly turned into a nightmare (Luke 15:11–32). The trouble with trouble is that it usually starts out as a whole lot of fun.

Sin has been around for a long time. It poked its ugly, fork-tongued head into the story before the ink dried on the first two chapters of Genesis. Although the story does not tell us what kind of fruit Adam and Eve ate that day or how many pieces they enjoyed before they realized they were not wearing their Hanes, it does remind us of Augustine's warning that sin comes when we take a perfectly natural desire or longing or ambition and try desperately to fulfill it without God. Not only is it sin; it is a perverse distortion of the image of God in us. All these good things, and all our security, are rightly found only and completely in God.

We seem to respond intuitively to sin just as Adam and Eve did—they hid in the bushes. We instinctively hide when confronted with our own sinful behavior.

A practical joker wrote up identical letters and put them in every mailbox in his small town. The letter read: "Guess what? I know what you are up to. I have proof and I'm going to bring it to the newspaper office thirty days from now. I hope you're satisfied. You'll get what you deserve." No name was signed. Over the next thirty days, there was no socializing at all in the friendly town. People refused to acknowledge waves or phone calls. A few prominent families put their homes up for sale and moved away.

Our initial reaction to sin is to hide. "Don't say anything about it and maybe they'll go away." Shame overwhelmed them. For the first time in their garden-fresh lives they could not stand scrutiny. It wasn't merely that they flinched when their partner's gaze dipped below neck; they had trouble looking into each other's eyes. The bushes served as a hiding place not only from God but also from each other.

If hiding doesn't work, we try deflecting our sin onto others. When someone confronts us with our sin, we deny the sin and feel anger at the accuser. Our nation saw this in action during the early stages of the Clinton debacle. He and his defenders pointed to anything but the truth. The blame was passed from mendacious women to a vast right-wing conspiracy.

A news magazine once reported that there is a kind of mirror system of morality in evil. People don't say, as they were more likely to do in past eras, that they are bad by nature. They make excuses like "It was necessary for me to do this; I had no choice. I didn't start it, but nobody's going to play me for a sucker." Cain blamed his brother Abel for God's disappointment in his sacrifice, and he killed him. The thief on the cross verbally abused Jesus. Pilate washed his hands of the matter and blamed it on Jesus' refusal to plead innocent. Often school bullies are taking out aggression felt as a result of parental abuse. From antisocial behavior in the workplace to domestic violence, deflected sin has become an art form for twenty-first-century citizens of the world. Global terrorism, church cover-ups of sexual abuse, sexist and racist attitudes in hiring are some of today's evils committed in the name of religion. Three centuries ago, Blaise Pascal said that people never do evil so completely and cheerfully as when they do it from religious convictions. Deflecting sin onto others or justifying our convictions in the name of God comes so naturally to us that often we can't see the sin even when it is right in front of us.

The other night I was watching the ABC evening news. Peter Jennings, with deep concern, reported that binge drinking on college campuses is at an all-time high. The consequences are tragic and no one seems to be able to curb the practice. The in-depth report said that drinking parties and happy hours have become so numerous in college neighborhoods that we need to hear an alarm ringing out for the safety and health of our young people.

Two hours later, on the same network, I watched *Spin City,* a show about the antics of the staff of the mayor of New York City. In this flashback episode Charlie, the deputy mayor, was meeting the mayor's other assistant, played by Heather Locklear, for the first time back in their college days. Charlie, a party dude who was always dressed in a leather jacket, crashes Locklear's stuffy political coffee and turns it into a drinking party, where everyone starts to have a great time. The lesson from the show is that drinking mass quantities of alcohol in college is the only way to have a really good time. Binge drinking, in other words, is the answer. The same social problem Peter Jennings preached about just two hours earlier was now being lifted up as the answer to a boring college life. The laugh track should have been added to the news.

I told my wife I should write to ABC News and point this out, but I am sure they would tell me I should write to the producers of *Spin City* and complain because they have no say in what they show on prime time. I never did write that letter.

We are really good at deflecting sin onto others. Yet occasionally there comes a moment when you and I realize that we have turned our backs on God's ways and find ourselves in trouble. We know we sin . . . . Yet . . . .

The apostle Paul put it this way:

> I obviously need help! I realize that I don't have what it takes. I can will it, but I can't *do* it. I decide to do good, but I don't *really* do it; I decide not to do bad, but then I do it anyway. My decisions, such as they are, don't result in actions. Something has gone wrong deep within me and gets the better of me every time.
>
> It happens so regularly that it's predictable. The moment I decide to do good, sin is there to trip me up. I truly delight in God's commands, but it's pretty obvious that not all of me joins in that delight. Parts of me covertly rebel, and just when I least expect it, they take charge.
>
> I've tried everything and nothing helps. I'm at the end of my rope. Is there no one who can do anything for me? Isn't that the real question?[20]

Others know we sin and fall short of the glory of God. In a class of eleven- and twelve-year-olds, a church school teacher intercepted a note being passed from a girl to a boy. It read, "I like you, too. But you sin too much." How often we can look sin in the face and not notice the danger looking back at us. A network news report a few years ago told about an unusual work of modern art: a chair affixed to a shotgun. People were to view it by sitting in the chair and looking directly into the barrel of the gun. The gun was loaded and set on a timer to fire at an undetermined moment within the next hundred years. The amazing thing was that people waited in line for a chance to sit and stare down the barrel of the shotgun. They all knew that the gun was loaded and could go off at any time, yet they sat down thinking that the fatal blast could not happen during their minute in the chair. That's how it is most of the time for us. Yet every once in a while we neither hide nor deflect our sin, but instead become aware that sin has invaded our life when we were not looking.

In 1991 a judge found two brothers, owners of a Connecticut wrecking company, guilty and fined them $900,000 for operating an illegal dump. In 1986, on an empty lot near their business, the brothers had started to store junk cars and parts. Over the years the junk piled up until there was a mountain of it over thirty-five feet high—over three stories! Looking back, it never was supposed to get that high.

That is what we say when we realize there is a pile of sins in our back yard. "It wasn't supposed to get this high." Similar thoughts have been around for a long time. Everyone's back yard is high with sins: "All have sinned and fallen short of the glory of God," said Paul in Romans. The prophet said, "Like sheep, we've all gone astray." "It was never supposed to get this high."

A British comic was interviewed on a Christian television show. In a surprising moment of candor, she said, "What I envy most about you Christians is your forgiveness. I have nobody to forgive me." We do. Jesus is his name. Confess to him your sins. Come clean. Admit you need forgiveness. Say, "Lord Jesus, I'm a sinner in need of a Savior." Accept his forgiveness and the grace-filled promise that you are forgiven for each one of your sins. And then promise to trust him with your life. The Bible says (in Rom. 4:7–8, paraphr.): "Happy are those whose wrongs are forgiven, whose sins are pardoned! Happy is the person whose sins the Lord will not keep account of!" Amen.

11
East of Eden
Genesis 3:23-24;
Romans 1:22-25; Isaiah 59:1-2

On the old television show *Hee Haw,* Doc Campbell is approached by a patient who says that he broke his arm in two places. The doc replies: "Well then, stay out of those places!" Somehow the old doc confused sin with something else. I don't want us to fall into the same trap. Question 11 of the contemporary catechism, *Belonging to God,* can help clear some things up about sin. However, knowing what sin is does not guarantee we will deal with it properly. Even at a very early age, we human beings tend to get confused when it comes to sin and how to deal with it.

At bedtime, a retired rabbi was telling his two grandsons a bedtime story. "Tonight we're going to hear a story about sin. Do you know what the word 'sin' means?" Seven-year-old Kevin spoke up: "It's when you do something bad." Four-year-old Aaron's eyes widened, and he said, "I know a big sin Kevin did today." Annoyed, Kevin turned to Aaron and said, "You take care of your sins, and I'll take care of mine." Now this may sound like a good way to deal with sin, but there is a better way.

Again, we may know what sin is, and that there are better ways to deal with it, but that doesn't guarantee we will or can avoid it. Nine traits or tendencies of human nature that can produce manifestations of sin today include materialism, pride, self-centeredness, laziness, anger, sexual desire, envy, gluttony, and lying. Not surprisingly, the contemporary list resembles the Ten Commandments, many of Jesus' warnings, the Seven Deadly Sins, and laws on the books of most states.

Adam and Eve couldn't avoid sinning. Going against the rules that God set down for them in the Garden, they turned their backs on God and bet their lives on a shaky promise by the one we call the Tempter. Their sin caused their mandatory relocation to a suburb just east of Eden, where they could do no more than eke out a living. Their relocation came about because God had given them the ability to decide things for themselves. Each of the nine vulnerabilities related to manifestation of sin has to do with choice and our freedom to choose. Since the Garden, humanity has habitually made bad choices. It seems to be in our genes. We are genetically programmed to be people with free will. Human existence is filled with instances and eras of unfairness mainly because we choose to let the nine Flash Points rule our choices. Humans have free will in matters of behavior, but like Adam and Eve, we have a tendency to make bad choices. One bad choice we make is to close God off from our lives.

Q. 11. What is sin?

A. 11. Sin is closing our hearts to God and disobeying God's law.

Sin is closing off one's life to the presence of God. Originally, when our first parents were forcibly relocated to east of Eden, God made the Garden of Eden a gated community, blocking their return. Those who lived outside could no longer enter the Garden. However, even though Jesus smashed down the gates with the cross, we place our own sin-made barriers at the entrance and keep ourselves out. The prophet Isaiah predicted this when he announced some six hundred years before Christ: "God's hand isn't too short to save you. God's ears aren't stopped up; God can hear you. But instead your sins have constructed a barrier between you and God, and your sins have hidden the Lord's face from you. The barriers you've built for yourself keep you from God" (Isa. 59:1–2, paraphr.).

Max Lucado, in his book *In the Eye of the Storm,* writes about how a human heart starts to close itself off to God. He equates our life to a window that is broken by a pebble. The pebble symbolizes bad news, a painful experience, an illness, or some other life-altering event. The pebble strikes the window and the crash echoes in the heart. The window shoots out a spider web of fragmented pieces. Lucado says that, suddenly, God is not easy to see.

> The view that had been so crisp had changed. You turned to see God, and his figure was distorted. It was hard to see him through the pain. It was hard to see him through the fragments of hurt. You were puzzled. God wouldn't allow something like this to happen, would he? . . . We look for God, but can't find him. Fragmented glass hinders our vision. . . . Lines jigsaw their way across his face. Large sections of the shattered glass opaque the view. And now you aren't quite sure what you see.[21]

When we close off our hearts to God, we make a choice either as a response to the pain of living in a fallen world or as an action intending to keep God out of our private affairs. In either case we close our hearts to God. And this is sin. Our address remains: East of Eden. Yet sin is more than this. According to Question 11 of the contemporary catechism, sin is not only closing our hearts to God, but also **disobeying God's law.**

There are some laws of nature we must obey, like gravity. One time a turtle wanted to join his friends the geese on their annual migration to Florida. But he knew that he could never make it on his own, so he asked a goose to help him. After some serious convincing, the goose agreed to take him along. The turtle told the goose to tie a rope to her leg, and the turtle took the rope in his mouth, and off they flew. The flight went fine until some people on the ground looked up in admiration and asked, "Who in the world thought of that?" Not being able to resist the chance to take the credit, the turtle opened his mouth to shout, "I diiiiiid . . . ."

The story points out how dangerous it is to ignore the laws that keep us safe, healthy, and alive. But what is even more important to our study, the turtle chose his action out of pride. God's laws are important for the well-being of ourselves and others. We are free to choose whether to follow them or not. Sin is choosing not to follow God's ways.

A Chicago minister tells a story about meeting a man who was deeply involved with the New Age movement for over five years. The minister asked, "What caused you to second-guess what you were involved in?" The man said, "It was the moral anarchy. I became part of a group and we used to sit around and talk about what 'my truth' was. One person would say, 'My truth is doing, saying, feeling, or acting out this form of morality.' And someone would say, 'Oh, that's nice. That's your truth. Well, this is my truth . . . .' "

The man got the idea that the wife he had been married to for many years was not as beautiful and wonderful as another woman in the group, who said that her truth was that they ought to get married. He said, "I thought about it more, and after a while I decided that was my truth, too. So we got our truth together. I divorced my wife. She was very upset about that, but I told her, 'Honey, this is my truth.' See! How are you going to argue with that?"

A short time later someone told this man about an innovative local church. He thought it was a New Age church. "That day," he told the pastor, "you gave a message about human beings standing morally accountable before a holy God. While you were talking I became conscious for the first time of my sin. I knew I was playing games. I was just making up the truth. That's all I was doing; manufacturing the truth I wanted for myself so I could live the way I wanted to live. The next morning I fell on my knees, and I received Christ and forgiveness."

The apostle Paul wrote two thousand years ago about people claiming to be smart despite their foolishness, thinking that they could do anything they wanted, no matter how immoral. Paul said they exchanged the truth about God for lies (Rom. 1:22–25). God made his ways clear to Adam and Eve, but they exchanged God's truth for a lie posed to them by the Tempter. Ignoring God's life-fostering ways is sin just as much as closing one's heart to God. In either case, we are all to some extent guilty of both. We need God's forgiveness. We need a better, more permanent way of dealing with our sin.

A local congregation had been hoping to build a new facility but chose instead to renovate a run-down building outside of town. After extensive remodeling work, the church was ready for business, with a new baptistery that was big enough to immerse a person fully underwater. But the building inspector wouldn't okay it, saying, "I can't, unless it has a separate septic tank." The deacons couldn't understand why a septic tank would be needed for a baptistery. The building inspector explained, "It's to avoid pollution in the ground." One of the deacons said with a sly smile, "I guess it would pollute, seeing that all those sins would be washed away!"

All of us have sinned and closed our hearts to God and disobeyed God's ways. May the Lord wash away all of our sin. The building inspector has approved your church for all manner of church activities . . . including the washing away of sins.

Q. 11. What is sin?

A. 11. Sin is closing our hearts to God and disobeying God's law.

Prayer: O gracious Lord: Yes, we have often closed you off from our lives and tried to keep a part of our life out of your control. Forgive us. We've closed off our hearts to you but ache to have you live there. Forgive us. We so often go against your commandments and think no one knows. But you do. Forgive us. We come up with our own truth to justify our sinful ways. We know that this is bogus. Forgive us. Your grace is awesome and we desire to seek first your ways in our lives. Amen.

12

Broken and Confused

Genesis 3:16-19; Ephesians 2:1-3

After working at the Amoco gas station for a week, I was scheduled to work Saturday night until closing. It was the perfect job for a college student. It was just down the street from our apartment. I worked afternoons until closing and was able to read and do homework when the station wasn't busy. This was in the "olden days" before self-service. I had to pump gas, clean windshields, check oil, inflate tires, add water, replace wiper blades, count the money each night, and hide it in a wooden box behind the counter, just as I had been told to do by the manager. After I locked up and left, the manager would come by and get the money and make a night deposit. All was going well. I was getting used to the work and I liked it.

Then Saturday came and I worked until closing. The day-shift guy handed over the money to me and asked if I knew what to do with it. I told him I would count it and hide it in the wooden box behind the counter just like I'd been doing all week. He said, "Fine." At closing time, I counted the money and hid it in the wooden box behind the counter. I locked up and went home.

On Sunday morning, I got a call from the owner to come down to the station because he needed to talk with me. He asked me for the money. I didn't have the money. I'd counted it and hidden it behind the counter in the wooden box as instructed. "But you weren't supposed to do that on Saturday night. The manager doesn't come in to do the night deposit on Saturday. You're supposed to take the money home with you and bring it in Monday," the owner scolded me. That is when I saw the policeman walk from behind the building with a notepad in his hand. The gas station had been robbed during the night. A panel on the bay door was kicked in and the hidden wooden box behind the counter was missing. The officer asked me a hundred questions and I answered them all the same way. I counted the money, hid it in a wooden box behind the counter, just like I was told to do. I explained that no one told me I should do anything different on Saturday night so I just counted the money and hid it in the wooden box behind the counter.

The owner called me over and said someone had to take responsibility for this. I suggested the manager, seeing that he didn't tell me to do anything different. The owner said I was the only one who knew there was money on the premises, so it looked like I would be the prime suspect. I told him that the day-shift guy, who had been working there for a long time, knew about my regimen of leaving the money under the counter for the manager to pick up later in the evening, but that he hadn't said anything about taking the money home instead. But I could tell that was not going to make a difference. He told me he could not have me arrested, seeing there was no proof, so instead he would have to fire me. I complained that I had done nothing wrong. In fact, I had done exactly what I was told to do. But my protest did no good. I was fired.

In a perfect world, this never would have happened. No commandments would break, no harm would be committed, no blame would be placed, and there would be no worries, no punishment, and no sin. In a perfect world, my word would be good enough to convince anyone that I was innocent. I would have continued to work at the Amoco gas station until I graduated from college and would have been able to do all my homework between the ding-dings of the bell. The policeman and owner should have believed me when I told them I did not do it. I should not have been punished for something I did not do. In a perfect world, something like this would never happen.

But we live in a world that is broken and confused by sin. Wrong is often confused with right. What is right is often treated as if it were wrong. Good folks get punished for doing nothing wrong while the guilty get away with murder. It seems justice goes to the highest bidder while injustice preys on the innocent and less fortunate. We hear of politicians using people as pawns, and warriors estimate *collateral damage* as if people were numbers on a computer readout. People believe lies, and truth is viewed as fairy tale. I should not have been fired. I was an innocent man. Yet in a fallen world, where sin confuses even the best of us, relationships break and trust vanishes as people think the worst and expect very little. When things go wrong, someone has to take the blame. When a commandment is broken, someone has to get fired.

By the way, there is a "rest of the story" as Paul Harvey used to say. I stopped by the gas station a few months later and heard that the guy working the day shift had been fired. It seems there was another Saturday night robbery. The wooden box from behind the counter went missing again. Vindicated! But nothing changed. No apology. No phone call with an offer of my old job back. I was still paying the price for breaking the Eighth Commandment that I did not break.

Things in this world are screwed up. Even when you are not guilty, you can end up paying for it just as if you really are. We live in a fallen world, where sin infects every aspect of life. Sin takes a heavy toll on relationships, self-esteem, and our dreams of a brighter future. We have no choice but to live with these limitations, the results of sin.

Q. 12. What are the results of sin?

**A. 12. Our relationship with God is broken. All our
relations with others are confused.**

The story of Adam and Eve is a story from prehistory passed down from generation to generation. It is an ancient campfire story that the Holy Spirit has kept intact for more years than we can count. Not much has changed in its telling, and its timeless truth points out some of humanity's harshest realities. Life in a world marred by sin is all screwy, confused, and broken. For the female, childbirth involves pain, yet the desire to be intimate with one's husband is strong. One causes the other. Pleasure leads to pain. What a world we live in! Tilling the dirt to provide for family will be super-difficult. The sweat of one's brow will be soothed only when the cool dirt is shoveled over one's lifeless body. Comfort comes only in death. What a screwy world we live in!

Augustine had it right when he said that we can find no rest until our hearts rest in God. Yet restless and empty hearts can be found in every household. Countless hearts ache for God's love, Christ's forgiveness, the Holy Spirit's direction. The connection between God and person is broken. The line is cut. The transmission is severed. The result of sin in human life is simply that we are cut off from God. Being cut off from the source of life brings death.

The apostle Paul, in Romans 6:23, said, "The wages of sin is death, but the free gift of God is eternal life in Christ Jesus our Lord." The word in New Testament Greek for "free gift" is the word for "grace." Broken relationships between people and God are mended when God's free gift of love is accepted and treasured in our hearts. Because we live in a world marred by sin, things get confused. People-to-people encounters are laden with harmful baggage of painful childhood memories, bruised egos, faltering self-esteem, failed career moves, debilitating memories of abuse, unforgiven sin, thoughtless prejudices, and personal chauvinism.

When we are in conversation with another person, psychologists tell us that we are talking not only with that person but are in unconscious ways also carrying on a conversation with people from our past or present, such as our boss, a parent, a bossy sibling, a mean teacher, a strict pastor, or an ex-spouse. We bring a carload of others to any conversation we have, and to every relationship we begin. Our relations with others are confused because we are not totally genuine with each other. Sin has marred even our most intimate moments.

As followers of Christ Jesus, we find that when our heart connects with God our lives begin to connect with others in God-inspired ways. One follows the other. Invite Christ into your heart and Christ will guide your relationships. When I teach the confirmation class at my church, I ask them to memorize a good portion of the contemporary catechism we are studying. At the conclusion of the class they recite the catechism for the church elders at a breakfast. When I come to Question 19, I ask, "What is the main point of the Ten Commandments?" They answer, "You shall love the Lord your God with all your heart, mind, and strength; and you shall love your neighbor as yourself." In other words, when our heart connects with God, our life begins to connect with others. Love God and let God into your heart, your mind, your strength. And then you'll find the ability and capacity to love your neighbor and love yourself.

The ancient story of Adam and Eve, a story told around campfires long before years were counted on calendars, clearly shows that people understood that our relationship with God is broken and that our relations with others are confused. It was also clear that no one wanted to live like that, with restless or empty hearts, lonely lives, and shallow love. So people looked for a way to reconnect with God and to love one another. The answer came to humankind in the person of Jesus, a carpenter from the small village of Nazareth. His message, his life, his amazing actions, his death, and his rising from the dead proved once and for all that life need not be broken and confused. We can open our hearts to God and be reconnected. And in doing so we can embrace others as brothers and sisters, no matter who they are, where they live, what holy book they read, or how they talk or look or sing. We are *challenged* to love God with all our heart, mind, and strength and our neighbors as ourselves.

Be connected to God in faith. Be connected to each other in love. Sin no longer dictates your life. Grace abounds. Amen.

13

Hate the Sin, Love the Sinner

Luke 19:1-10; 2 Corinthians 5:17-21

Our tour bus rounded a corner in our driver's usual "hurry up to get there" style. John, our Palestinian Christian guide, pointed out a small, fenced-in park with an old tree in its center. He announced that it was a sycamore tree. We were returning from a visit to the archaeological site of Jericho, the oldest city in the world, as some estimate. The sycamore tree was planted by the local Palestinians for the sake of Christian tourists who came looking for the tree that Zacchaeus climbed to get a good look at Jesus. Our guide explained that the tree was old, but not that old. The best guess is that it was about three hundred years old. Of course, no one can say for sure if that is actually the location of the tree Zacchaeus climbed, but it does prove that sycamore trees grow in that region. I hope I can say the same thing—I planted a sycamore tree in the front yard of the church I serve so that our children can see the kind of tree that the Danny DeVito–sized man, Zacchaeus, climbed the day Jesus came to town.

Our contemporary catechism, *Belonging to God,* uses Zacchaeus's story to illustrate Question 13.

Q. 13. How does God deal with us as sinners?

Zacchaeus was a model sinner. He was a Jew who worked for the Roman government, collecting taxes and tariffs in the border town of Jericho, which is located at the site of a convergence of ancient trade routes. Observant Jews despised revenue agents for several good reasons.

First, for a political reason: they worked for Gentiles in a job that took money out of the pockets of hard-working Israelites.

Second, for reasons of cleanliness: tax collectors touched money and paperwork and interacted with Gentiles. A good Jew did not physically touch Gentiles or their possessions.

Third, for an ethical reason: tax collectors made their money by skimming a percent of the tax dollar to keep for themselves. The more they could skim, the more they pocketed.

Fourth, for a religious reason: tax collectors brokered in the Roman coin, on which was engraved the image of the Emperor, who claimed to be a god. This was blasphemy against God and a transgression against the First and Second Commandments.

Finally, for a social reason: tax collectors usually socialized with other outcasts and sinners.

Zacchaeus, therefore, was not on the "A list" of Jericho's Jewish society. Luke tells us that he was the chief tax collector of the region. As people rise to the pinnacle of a profession that is corrupt, the higher they climb, the greater is their culpability and complicity. Zacchaeus was in it deeper than all the guilty Enron executives combined, which may be the reason he put aside his dignity, lifted his tunic and climbed the sycamore tree.

He heard that someone was coming to town who loved sinners. Someone was coming his way who rattled the establishment because he bent his elbow with a few tax collectors now and then. Someone was up the road who just possibly might have a good word for him. Someone was walking toward him who might be able to save a lost soul, a soul that was about to burst if things didn't change soon.

Annie Dillard in *Pilgrim at Tinker Creek* tells a story about a frog. The green frog was half in and half out of the water. Its eyes were wide but dull. As she was looking at it, the frog began to sag like a deflated bag. The head collapsed like a tent that had been kicked in. A giant water bug hung over the frog. Dillard describes the aggressor and its action as a large, heavy insect. It eats insects, tadpoles, fish, and frogs. Its grasping forelegs are mighty and hooked inward. It seizes a victim with these legs, hugs it tight, and paralyzes it with enzymes injected during a vicious bite. Through the puncture shoots the poison that dissolves the victim's muscles and bones and organs—all but the skin—and through it the giant water bug sucks out the victim's body, reduced to juice.[22]

Like a giant water bug, sin can suck the life out of us. "Zacchaeus was a wee little man," the children's song goes. We can add another verse to the Sunday school song that would go like this:

> Zacchaeus was like a hollow frog,
> a hollow frog was he.
> He hopped right up a sycamore tree,
> lost he was found to be.
> And Jesus said, "Zacchaeus, I hate your sin,
> but I will never stop loving you.
> And I'm giving you new life today."

Q. 13. How does God deal with us as sinners?
A. 13. God hates our sin but never stops loving us.

It was over a hundred years ago that traveling evangelist Dwight L. Moody coined the familiar phrase "Hate the sin, but love the sinner." This is how God deals with us. Jesus knew about Zacchaeus. How could he not? Can you imagine the scene? A main street, civic and church dignitaries, crowds, a parade, children standing on tiptoes, children running, their parents running after them, older brothers letting little sisters sit on their shoulders to see the famous Jesus of Nazareth. Among this crowd was the town's number-one scoundrel, a small, old man wedged solidly in a fork between two branches about six feet high. Jesus knew, long before he reached the spot, just who that small-hearted man was. I am sure everyone made sure he knew who he was and exactly what they thought of him.

So it wasn't a surprise that Jesus said to Zacchaeus: "I'm dining with you for lunch." There's only one logical reason he was up in the tree: to get noticed! Jesus noticed—of course (he loves the sinner)—and everything changed for Zacchaeus because Jesus hates sin. And Zacchaeus realized he had to change the way he lived his life if he had any hope of accepting the love that was coming his way.

God loves you just the way you are, but God loves you too much to leave you that way! For Zacchaeus, the old had passed away, and all things were new (2 Cor. 5:7).

As Christians we take our cue from Jesus, who hates the sin but loves the sinner. C. S. Lewis, in his Christian primer *Mere Christianity,* said that he remembered Christian teachers telling him he must hate the actions of a bad person rather than the person. He used to think that this was a silly way to deal with sin until he realized that he acted this way toward one particular sinner—himself. However much he might dislike his own sinful behavior and attitudes, he continued to love himself. There had never been the slightest difficulty about it. Just because he loved himself, he was sorry to find that he was the sort of person who did those things.

> Consequently, Christianity does not want us to reduce by one atom the hatred we feel for cruelty and treachery. We ought to hate them. Not one word of what we have said about them needs to be unsaid. But it does want us to hate them in the same way in which we hate things in ourselves: being sorry that the man should have done such things, and hoping, if it is anyway possible, that somehow, sometime, somewhere, he can be cured and made human again.[23]

Lewis was touching on another of Jesus' radical ideas: the idea of loving one's neighbor as one loves oneself. But we have to admit that it is a difficult challenge, especially as we think about terrorists, criminals, and misguided dictators. It may also encourage some of us to reconsider things like capital punishment, the "one strike and you're out" policies, mandatory sentencing, and all the other societal solutions that throw grace out with the bath water. After all, all of us love second chances, opportunities to be forgiven, and the confidence that the gospel promise has come true, that the old is gone and the new life has begun.

Thus, in learning how God deals with us as sinners, we also learn how we can relate to others who have sinned against us; we learn to hate the sin but to love the sinner.

14

People with a New Beginning

Isaiah 11:1-3; Romans 9:4-5

Q. 14. What did God do to help us?

A. 14. God chose the people of Israel to make a new beginning. They received God's covenant and prepared the way for Jesus to come as our Savior.

One of the things I love about my job as a minister is that I can do fun things and call it work. Our church's annual rafting trip down the James River, Youth Club visits to Busch Gardens, Men's Group nights at the Norfolk Tides baseball games all count as being on the job for me. In June our church will once again start up its Tuesday Afternoon Fellowship Golf. At 4:30 I'll join members of my church on one of the challenging golf courses in our community for nine or eighteen holes of "Christian fellowship and pastoral interaction." With these kinds of benefits, I'm surprised seminaries are not bursting at the seams with eager candidates for ministry!

Golf is a game of covenants, which are promises or contracts. To play golf, you have to contract to play by the rules. The late Dick Payne, one of the best senior golfers of his day in Virginia, told me that the first thing I need to do to be a good golfer is to buy a rule book and follow it. I am not a good golfer yet, as I have not purchased a rule book, but I will someday. Golf is a game in which you contract with yourself and promise others you will play by a set of rules, either your own or the official USGA rules. The promise to play by the rules of the game, and the personal contract among golfers to keep that commitment in the forefront on each of eighteen holes, is what gives golf its meaning, purpose, and pleasure. Without these promises, golf makes no sense; indeed, it becomes a good walk spoiled.

Our study of the contemporary catechism has brought us to the theological question of what God has done to help human beings live godly lives, both individually and in community. We have discovered so far that God loves us even though we are far from perfect. We are made in God's image with the ability and challenge to live for God and to care for the world that God has created for us to live in. We are sinners, but forgiven sinners. (Thanks be to God!) As such, we know that God will somehow help us overcome the limitations of our human nature in order to find meaning, purpose, and pleasure in a God-inspired life. And it is at this point in the contemporary catechism that our attention is directed to a lasting promise that God made over four thousand years ago in the Middle Bronze Age.

A man from the ancient land called Ur (in what is now Iraq) received a promise from God that if he and his family moved from his home and trusted God to lead them to a new land, God would make him the progenitor of a new people, a people who were not only blessed by God, but who would also bless the world on God's behalf (Gen. 12:1–3). His name was Abram, later to become Abraham, and he was married to Sarah.

The divine promise was repeated to Abraham and Sarah's son, and to Isaac and Rebecca's son, and to Jacob and his wives' sons—and again four hundred years later to their descendant Moses and then to Joshua and David and the prophets. God promised to bless them and to make them a blessing to all the people of the world. The initial promise, or *covenant*, was one-sided and irrevocable. It was a promise that God would be with this people no matter what. This made them the chosen people of God. It was a promise that would be kept even when it would make sense not to keep it.

A few years ago, my family had a wonderful time celebrating my son Peter's graduation from Syracuse University. The commencement speaker was former New York City mayor Rudy Giuliani. He told a story that reminds me of the kind of promise or covenant that God has made with his people, a promise to be kept even when it would make sense not to keep it. The mayor told about one firefighter's courage on 9/11. The firefighter had been injured on the job on the September 10. At 8 A.M. the next day he went to the doctor's office for an appointment. The doctor determined that he was not to go back to work for several weeks because of his injuries. As the doctor was delivering his prognosis, he heard the news of the attack on the World Trade Center.

The firefighter was in Brooklyn at the time. He was told to go home and not to report to work. Instead, he went to a firehouse in Brooklyn, vacant because all the firefighters had been dispatched to the World Trade Center. He went to a locker and borrowed another firefighter's turnout gear. He left a note. In it, he explained who he was and why he had taken the gear. As an afterthought, he wrote in the note: "Please tell my mother and father that I love them very much and that I owe everything to them, and tell my sister that I love her," then he signed his name. This is a man who had gone to thousands of fires and had never written a note before.

The mayor imagined that as the firefighter drove across the Brooklyn Bridge he surely felt as though he was driving into hell. That's what one saw from there, an inferno unlike anything one could possibly describe. The firefighter had every reason to turn back. He was injured. He wasn't supposed to be working. He was driving into a death zone. No one would ever criticize him if he turned around and went back, but he drove on to Ground Zero. He went into the first tower, and saved two people from the fire. He entered the tower a second time, right before it collapsed. The firefighter died.[24]

This firefighter had made a promise to protect and serve the people of his city the day he put on his FDNY uniform. Even though he had every reason to set aside that promise for a moment, he did not—and it cost him his life.

Century after century, God has constantly had good reason to set aside the promise that God will be with us, to bless and keep us, and never to withdraw divine love and grace. Twenty-seven times in the Old Testament the Hebrew word we translate as "abandoned" is used to describe how the people closed their hearts and minds to God. But in spite of every good reason to set aside the promise, we hear the Lord, over and over again, say: "Remember now, I'll be at your side and I'll keep you safe wherever you go. . . . I will not leave you . . . and that I promise" (Gen. 8:15, paraphr.). Even when there was every reason to forget about the promise, God did not, and it cost God his life. You see, God eventually expressed God's love for the world by sending his only Son, Jesus the Christ, to demonstrate once and for all just how deep and how wide and how gracious God's love really is. This divine action was to show God's determination to keep his promise that no matter what happens, God will not leave us or abandon us. This is both an Old Testament and a New Testament promise that God will never break. (Deut. 31:6; Heb. 13:5). Paul put it this way: "If God is for us, who can be against us? Who then can separate us from the love of Christ? Can trouble do it, or hardship or persecution or hunger or poverty or danger or death? I'm convinced that neither death, nor life, nor angelic powers, nor earthly rulers, nor things now, nor things to come, nor anything else in all creation will be able to separate us from the love of God in Christ Jesus, our Lord" (Rom. 8:31–39, paraphr.).

God selected a family from an obscure town and made Abraham and Sarah covenant partners. God would bless them, and God offered them the chance to bless the world by sharing God with everyone. Although time after time the people of the covenant let God down, God still kept the promise and found ways to remind the people that it was irrevocable. God would not abandon his people. Eventually God sent his own Son to demonstrate the lengths God was willing to go to in order to make this promise clear. Jesus' life, death, and resurrection restated the promise in global terminology; it is called the *new promise* or, biblically speaking, the new covenant.

On the Jewish agricultural holiday of Pentecost, God marked the beginning of the New Testament—the new community of promise—by sending God's Holy Spirit to empower believers to live as if the promise is and will always be true. And the promise remains the same for the church today. No matter what happens in life or how things work out for us or where God leads us on our journey, "nothing, no, not a thing, is able to separate us from the love of God" (see Rom. 8:38–39). Some of us, more than others, need to hear this promise today. Some people are going through very tough moments right now. Some situations are so private that no one else knows the turmoil that is about to break in. But we are to remember the meaning of Romans 8:38–39: "Nothing, no, not a thing, is able to separate you from the love of God." Some are just hanging on to the barest of threads. Faith has been stretched so thin that it is down to a single monofilament strand, and the main prayer is that somehow God will not let it snap. Remember: "Nothing, no, not a thing, is able to separate you from the love of God."

As with Abraham, experiences such as military deployment, job hunting, retirement, trial separations, or a troubling diagnosis may be taking you or a loved one away from home or the people you love. It is a traumatic, heart-wrenching, and faith-testing time today, just as it was for Abraham and Sarah. And you wonder if God is in the move and will sustain you and lead you to a place that is right for you. Remember: "Nothing, no, not a thing, is able to separate you from the love of God." Despite the uncertainty of the present and the future, this promise—this covenant—will sustain you. Hold on to it!

One of the Coast Guard families in my church moved to northern Virginia. The family had been a major force in the church, but God had a change in store for them. Writing in the church newsletter to say goodbye, Jim and Katrina wrote:

> We have prayed so hard for God to keep us here but God has a plan for us. We are so thankful that he brought us here; we have truly experienced the growth and love of a church family. Now we must thank God for our new journey as we move to a new home. The hardest part about leaving is St. Andrew and its members. In four years, we have seen tremendous growth, love, concern, and fellowship between church members and we are so thankful to have been a part of it. We do not want to say goodbye, but just "see you later." May the Lord watch between you and me when we are absent one from the other.

This is what holding on to the promise looks like in real life. The promise has empowered generations of believers for over four thousand years to believe that no matter what happens, nothing can separate us from the love of God in Christ Jesus our Lord. May it guide your life as well.

15

A Promise Forever and Ever

Romans 11:29; Hebrews 8:10

Watch what you promise! A local businessman ran for state representative from his district, using as a campaign slogan the words "I will work for you!" His commercials played hundreds of times on radio and TV stations. The slogan was plastered on billboards, and thousands of leaflets were handed out containing the bold promise "I will work for you!"

He was elected, and shortly afterward he received a call from a farmer in his district, who told him that because he had voted for him he was taking him up on his offer. The farmer told the congressman that he needed some help putting up his hay. The politician could think of nothing to say in response, so he went to the man's farm and helped him put up his hay. He remarked that he was going to have to watch what he promised!

Watch what you promise, especially if it affects someone else. After an evening out, the parents came home and found their children asleep in their beds. Usually, when left with a babysitter, the kids ran wild and never were settled down before the parents came home. But this night, they were fast asleep in their own beds. As the babysitter walked out the door, she said, "By the way, I promised the children that if they would stay in bed, you would buy them a pony in the morning." Watch what you promise, especially if it affects someone else.

Long ago, God made a promise to humankind through a man named Abraham. This covenant has held for four thousand years, since the Middle Bronze Age! And we can be sure it will hold forever and ever. God promised Abraham an eternal covenant:

"On that day, the LORD made a covenant with Abram, saying, 'To your descendants I give this land . . . ' " (Gen. 15:18). "As for me, this is my covenant with you: You shall be the ancestor of a multitude of nations" (Gen. 17:4).

God promised to bless and protect and to be faithful at other times, too. To Noah God promised, "This is the sign of the covenant that I make between me and you and every living creature. . . . I have set my bow in the clouds, and it shall be a sign of the covenant between me and the earth" (Gen. 9:12, 13). And to King David: "I have made a covenant with my chosen one, I have sworn to my servant David: 'I will establish your descendants forever ' " (Ps. 89:3, 4a).

The apostle Paul understood God's special promise to be eternal. As he said in Romans, "[F]or the gifts and the calling of God are irrevocable" (Rom. 11:29). God's covenant is a *forever* promise, something we can count on for sure.

Q. 15. What is the covenant?

A. 15. The covenant is an everlasting agreement between God and Israel.

The word *covenant* comes from a Hebrew verb meaning "to fetter," which means to chain or lock things together. As the language developed, *covenant* became a term to describe an agreement between persons or villages. Later on, the term came to represent a binding contract, cut in stone. Today one might hear, "It's not set in stone," in reference to an agreement that is only penciled in, so to speak. If you pencil something in, it is not permanent. I do that a lot when people call, wondering if they can get married at the church I serve. I have learned in twenty-five years of ministry to pencil in the wedding until I get their paperwork and their commitment to a date and time. Only then do I use ink to mark the date. Only then is it set "in stone."

This meaning of the word derives from the ancient peoples of Mesopotamia. "Cutting a deal" literally meant "cutting it in stone." Chiseling hieroglyphics in stone and cutting cuneiform letters in a tablet of clay were the writing mediums of the day. A contract or a promise was called a "word." To write a "word" meant to write a contract in stone. A word cut in stone is a promise forever and ever. God's promises are cut in stone.

When Moses came down from Mt. Sinai with a tablet in each arm, the words were cut in stone. The Decalogue (or the "Ten Words") is meant to be our side of the promise. To love the Lord with all our heart, soul, and strength and our neighbor as ourselves summarizes the Decalogue, which we know as the Ten Commandments.

For the Hebrews—including Noah, Abraham and Sarah, Moses—the covenant is the foundation of devotion to one God. God promised to be faithful and just, merciful and loving, and God required the people to worship the Lord alone, to show justice and mercy, and to walk humbly in love (Mic. 6:8). The covenant between God and the people of Israel was the beginning of monotheism (the worship of one God) in the world. And we continue that style of worship today, thousands of years later. God promises to be faithful and just, merciful and loving; our promise to God is to love God and to love neighbor. Moses, Joshua, the prophets, Jesus, and Paul all share this basic subtext in each of their stories that we find in Scripture. God's promises are forever, and our promise is to love God and neighbor.

When we gather at the Lord's Table, we reenact the sacred covenant. In the Greco-Roman world of the first century, cutting a contract did not require chiseling in stone or making an indent in a slab of clay. And it would be another two thousand years before the term "penciling in an appointment" or the practice of beaming Palm Pilot appointments back and forth would be used. Instead, making a toast with wine sealed a promise in Greco-Roman days. It was a legal symbol of a binding agreement. It is possible that Jesus mixed the Jewish custom of the Passover Cup of Salvation with the Greco-Roman official toast of libations to declare the *New* Covenant—the new agreement or promise—that Jesus is, in fact, God's Son, sent to express God's deepest intentions.

The covenant expressed at the Lord's Table also symbolizes the basic subtext that runs throughout the Bible. This is the promise that God will be faithful and just, merciful and loving, and that we as God's people are to love God with all our heart, soul, and strength and our neighbor as ourselves. The bread broken and the cup shared include you and me in the drama of God's forever promise. With the lifting of the cup and the tasting of the sweet liquid, the promise is sealed. God, in Jesus Christ and through the electric presence of the Holy Spirit, expresses love for us and will always love us. God, in Jesus Christ, will be with us no matter what happens. We can count on it.

With the lifting of the cup and the tasting of its sweet liquid, we promise to lift high the name of the one true God and to love our neighbor in the way we would like to be loved. Although we often break our end of the promise, God never breaks a promise. And to add glory to grace, God even forgives our unfaithfulness and renews the New Covenant with us every time we lift the cup and experience the love of Father, Son, and Holy Spirit.

16

God's Love, Our Banner

Genesis 17:1-7;
Galatians 3:14; 1 Peter 2:9-10

Whenever someone announces that she is having a baby, I cannot help thinking that a baby is God's way of telling the world that God's not done with us yet. At the same time, I want to warn those so warm and safe in a mother's womb: "Life's not for cowards! It's a scary and uncertain place out here. You're warm, safe, and loved in there. Out here can be cold, dark, threatening, and lonely. The world is not for the weak-hearted. You'll need God to make it."

A problem I see is that human beings are by nature self-centered. That character flaw blinds humanity to the reality of how things really are. Human beings carry the Adam trait, a flaw in our character passed on to us from our original parents. It sends a signal to the brain that we can handle anything on our own. We do not need God.

The blame game since 9/11 continues to prove that we think we can handle our scary and uncertain world all by ourselves. Blaming 9/11 on the FBI, the CIA, or the White House is naive. One hears politicians say that if we had only connected the dots in the right order back then, we could have prevented the terrorist attacks and avoided going to war. If we had only had better communication between agencies, none of this evil would have happened. If we only had worked harder at intelligence or had spies on the ground, we would be safe today from the sins of humanity. We just did not do all we could have done to prevent it. According to this argument, if we had done a better job, I would not be afraid to fly. I would not feel so uncertain about the future, or so uneasy about my neighbor. If we could only fix the blame on "the someone" who let us down, then we might be satisfied that events are not out of our control or that evil will not hurt us again or that we can be safe from the sins of humanity. If we can fix the blame on that "someone" who let us down, then we can rest assured that all is under control. It was just a mistake, a foul-up, a glitch, a technical malfunction of the system. In other words, we should be able to handle it without God's help. The patron saint of our day must be Cleopatra, the "Queen of de Nile"!

By nature, we are blind to the reality that we human beings cannot do it alone, although we really try hard to do so. But the truth is that in a scary and uncertain world, a world where life is not for the weak-hearted, we really need God. Yet some will totally ignore this and live as if God does not exist. They can handle life on their own, thank you very much! "Fools say in their hearts, 'There is no God' " (Ps. 14:1).

You probably never heard of Colin Rizzio, who took the math SAT exam a few years ago when he was a high school senior. Colin marked his answer D to a question, but changed it when he realized that it could be A or D. He checked it out with his math teacher later and they both agreed the test had made a mistake. They contacted the Educational Testing Service, in Princeton, which makes up the SATs, and sure enough, Colin was right. There had not been an error in the SAT tests since 1982. The test designers were embarrassed. They had made an assumption that an exponent was a positive. Colin saw that it could easily be a negative and that this would affect the answer. Wrong assumptions on an SAT test can shave a few points off a student's score, but wrong assumptions about life and God are dangerous. One common assumption is that we can handle life all on our own. The foolish say in their hearts, "We don't need God." But we do. Our Creator knows this and promises to be there for us every moment of every day, because without God we are nothing. The Bible calls this promise a covenant. Another word for covenant is agreement. Our contemporary catechism explains it in some detail.

Q. 16. What is in this agreement?

A. 16. When God called Abraham and Sarah, God promised to bless their family, which was later called Israel. Through the people of Israel, God vowed to bless all the peoples of the earth. God promised to be Israel's God, and they promised to be God's people. God vowed to love Israel and to be their hope forever, and Israel vowed to worship and serve only God.

As Christians, we are included in this agreement through Jesus Christ, a son of Abraham. It was God's intention that "in Christ Jesus the blessing of Abraham might come to the Gentiles, so that we might receive the promise of the Spirit through faith" (Gal. 3:14). We may not be related by blood to Abraham as Jesus was, but that does not matter. We still are included in the promises because Christ lives in us. Like the Old Testament church, the New Testament church experiences the love and care promised by God through the covenant.

When things get rough, God promises to protect us. I found myself interested in a television program explaining life on the oil rigs in the North Sea and the Gulf of Mexico. In case of a fire or hurricane, the workers climb into a rescue capsule that looks like a yellow school bus. They strap themselves in; then when the entry port is sealed, the vehicle is released down a chute and propelled away from the rig. Harnesses protect the workers from the brutal impact when the capsule hits the water. The capsule rights itself and bobs in the sea until rescue craft come and pick up those inside. This illustration can remind us that even our best inventions are not fail-safe. An oil rig may fall over in the hurricane, but those in the right place, whether physically in a rescue capsule or spiritually in Christ, are saved from the ultimate consequences of the storm. The storm will run its course in time. The welfare of the workers depends on whether they are in the rescue device or not. For Christians, the outcome depends on whether we are in Christ or not. God's love forms a safe refuge when things get rough. This is a biblical promise.

God also promises not to stop loving us even when we push the promise aside. God is relentless in loving us. Back in 1981, police were staging an intensive search for a stolen Volkswagen Beetle and the thief who stole it. They had to find the car, fast. Announcements ran on the radio to try to contact the thief. On the front seat of the stolen car sat a box of crackers that, unknown to the thief, were laced with rat poison. The car owner had planned to use the crackers as rat bait. Now the police and the owner of the Volkswagen were more interested in catching the thief in order to save his life rather than to retrieve the car. So often, when we find ourselves running from God, we think God is out to get us. In reality, however, God is reaching out to protect us and save us from hurting ourselves. We think we are running away from a mean God, but in fact we are eluding a rescue. God has promised to love us, bless us, and keep us safe even when we may not feel worthy of such an expression of love.

As they were driving to the movies, Rob asked his future wife, "Tell me, honey, have you ever been in love before?" She thought for a minute and answered, "No. I once respected a man I dated for his brilliant mind. I dated a firefighter, and I admired him because he was so brave. I was in awe of one of the boys I dated because he was absolutely good-looking. But with you, well, how else can I explain it, except love?"

How else can we explain God's affection for human beings, except love? That is the subtext of every chapter in the Bible. Although we may not deserve it, God loves us and promises to bless us, care for us, guide us, and forgive us. God promises to be our God and to keep us close as God's own people.

At first glance, the people of God look ordinary. We tend to be a collection of Homer Simpsons, Charlie Browns, and Lucille Balls, with an occasional Mother Teresa or St. Francis thrown in. Thus, it is hard for us to take the apostle Peter seriously when he showers the people of God with an array of accolades that seem to be based on wishful thinking rather than grounded in reality: "A chosen race, a royal priesthood, a holy nation, God's own people" (1 Peter 2:9a). That's a stretch, some critics might say.

If you take a cursory look at the church, you might come to the conclusion that we are a collection of nobodies, but God must see something else when God sees the church. "God don't make junk," the bumper sticker reads. Maybe that is what Peter was trying to say. Maybe Peter wants us to see ourselves as God sees us, as a royal, holy, chosen people, worthy to be loved.

Nothing is random about being the church. Nothing is generic or plain. We are God's people, human beings who are worth loving, persons for whom God was willing. And a community able to understand this is blessed so as to be a blessing. Peter says it this way, "We're God's people in order that we may proclaim the mighty acts of God" (1 Peter 2:9b, paraphr.). In other words, God picked you to show and tell God's love.

God shows no "favorites" here. Rather, God chooses each one of us to serve God by doing God's work in the world. As a teacher taps those she wants to help her with work that needs to be done, so God taps each one of God's people, making us worthy.

God is choosing you for a certain purpose in the world today. An invisible hand is on your shoulder. . . . Do you feel it?

17

God Leads, We Follow

Exodus 15:13; Joshua 1:1–3; Hebrews 11:29–31

God is always communicating with us in order to make us aware of God's ways. One time God wrote out a message on the wall of the king's palace in Babylon: *Mene, mene, tekel, parsin* (Dan. 5:25). No one in the kingdom could read these words. The brightest minds of the day tried to decipher them, but the words were not understood, even by the wisest scholars.

Did you hear the one about the pharmacist who blew himself up? He was in the back room of the drugstore mixing a prescription for a woman, when "bam!" He staggered out of the room, lab coat on fire and hair singed. He said to the woman, "Would you mind asking your doctor to write out the prescription again, but this time, to print it?" Maybe if God *printed*, the king would have been able to read the writing on the wall, which said that the king's life had been weighed in the balance and found wanting (Dan. 5:27).

It should be a simple thing for us to discern God's will, but time and again, God has to work doubly hard to make divine ways known to us.

A father got upset about the time it took for his six-year-old son to get home from his friend's house just a block away. He figured that he would find out for himself just how long it took to walk it. Just eight minutes! But the boy took so long to get home—sometimes over a half hour. The father decided to find out just what took him so long, so he called the neighbor and asked to have his son sent home in ten minutes. The father walked around the block and then followed his son home. The father discovered that eight minutes was plenty of time for a grown-up to walk that distance, but it was not enough time for a six-year-old. He failed to take into consideration such important things as side trips to track down a column of ants, or a stop to watch a lady change a tire, or to run a stick along a picket fence, or to try to catch a squirrel's tail. In short, the father had forgotten what it was like to be six years old.

Although it should be a simple thing, God knows that it takes us a bit longer than it should to catch on to what God is trying to do in our lives and in our world. God knows what it is like to be human. God created us. God even became a human being, walking in our shoes for thirty-three years. God knows that it takes a bit longer for us to catch on to what God wants for us, to hear God's voice in prayer, to discover his ways in Scripture, or to see what God is up to in nature. God knows we need more than just a one-time event to make us aware of what God wants us to do. It seems that God knows we are half-an-hour people in an eight-minute world. It takes us a bit longer to catch on.

The seventeenth question of the contemporary catechism, *Belonging to God*, points to this:

Q. 17. How did God keep this covenant?

A. 17. God led Israel out of slavery in Egypt, gave them the Ten Commandments through Moses, and brought them into the land that God had promised.

God led them out of slavery. . . . God gave them the commandments. . . . God brought them into the Promised Land. If you think about it, any one of these three earth-shaking events should have been enough to solidify a relationship and trust with God forever. And that is not counting the flood, Sarah's pregnancy, two persons created from clay, or creation itself! But Israel took a long time to catch on. God remained faithful to the people nonetheless, continually providing new insights into God's ways and challenging Israel to be a chosen people. God kept finding ways to make them aware of the covenant God had made with the people of faith.

Our Jewish cousins remember the Exodus every Passover. This one event solidified the Hebrew religion and the Jewish people. *God led and the people followed.* The Exodus event shook the world by showing that God was stronger than the strongest army a nation could muster. It should have been enough to prove that God was the One worth trusting.

Yet God knows us all too well. When the people of Israel once again needed to be reminded of God's intention for them, the Lord called Moses up to a mountain and sent him down with Ten Commandments etched in stone. Smoke and fire engulfed them, the ground shook, lightning flashed, and God spoke. God wrote out (in plain Hebrew!) what God wanted the faithful to do and who they were called to be.

One would think that this would be enough to convince human beings, at least the Hebrews, that God is so concerned for them that God would even write instructions for us to see. " 'I am your God. I brought you out of the land of Egypt, out of slavery, and gave you your freedom. And I am your God; these are the instructions for living a lifestyle that honors me,' said the Lord" (Ex. 20:2, paraphr.).

You would think that would have been enough, but still, as human beings they needed to hear more. So God brought the faithful into the land of promise. The Jordan River parted, in much the same way as the Red Sea did, to let the people in. Walls tumbled as trumpets held on a major chord. Enemies fled at every report that the Hebrews were approaching. Abraham's people were home again and this time God let them stay. The land once promised to Abraham and Sarah in the covenant was now their home. It really was the land of promise for the people of God!

Today there are many who say that the Promised Land is symbolic rather than a piece of land. Street battles are being fought between religious peoples today by some who say the land is divinely promised to them, while others say that the land is just *land* and they want their homes back. For the descendants of ancient Israel, the struggle to live in the Promised Land is a life-and-death matter. For Christians, the land of promise is not located on a map of the Middle East, but is a location that is fluid, moving with us wherever we find ourselves. Unlike the ancient tabernacle, it does not need to be packed up each night. The land of promise does not fit into a backpack or a lunch box. It is too amorphous to put in the trunk of a car but it is not too big to encompass the heart. For those who are Christ's followers, the land of promise is not a physical place, but a spiritual dimension in which we live out the covenant God has made with us.

The land of promise is the place in our lives where God keeps showing God's self to us. It is the part of our life in which God keeps probing our spiritual depths and calling us to holy living. It is the moments when we sense that God is genuine and that we are truly God's people. It is the place in our lives where we discern the presence of God, and we come to know that God is real.

God brings us into the land of promise . . . where we are forgiven . . . and where we can forgive.

In a story of Jimmy Carter's campaign for president against Ronald Reagan in 1980, a newspaper story by David Willis of the *New York Times* reported that Reagan had won an important television debate. Willis attributed Reagan's victory to columnist George Will's happening upon a copy of Carter's debate notes and passing them on to the Reagan camp. Reagan went on to win the election.

Carter never forgot what George Will did to him. In a 1997 interview, Carter said that as he was teaching forgiveness in his Sunday school class, he tried to go through his memory and think of persons he resented or had not forgiven. George Will was one of those people. Carter wondered what he and Will had in common and came up with baseball. Will had written a book on the subject and Carter had refused to read it. He went to the store and bought a used copy, paying a dollar for it. After he read it, Carter wrote Will a note and told him the truth of his resentful feelings toward Will and how he had found his book delightful. He wrote that he hoped that they might permanently be reconciled. Will wrote back a nice, humorous note, seemingly accepting Carter's offer of reconciliation. He said that his only regret was that Carter did not pay full price for the book![25]

Anyone can hold a grudge. It takes a person with a malleable character living in the land of promise to initiate reconciliation and forgiveness

God brings us into the land of promise, where justice comes sometimes by roundabout ways.

An old Jewish folktale tells of a time when a boy was found murdered. The authorities arrested a local troublemaker, believing that they could not only solve the murder but also rid the town of this troublemaker once and for all. After a questionable trial, the judge suggested that the guilt of the man be determined using the ancient tradition of drawing lots. The judge would put two pebbles in a bowl. If the man picked a white pebble, he would be set free. If he picked a black one, he would be executed. The judge bent down and picked up two pebbles and put them in the bowl. But the man suspected that the judge had set a trap for him by putting two black pebbles in the bowl, so as he drew the pebble, he dropped it on the ground, where it disappeared among the stones and dirt. "You are not only a criminal, but you are clumsy," the judge said. "We'll have to do it over again." "Not at all," the man said. "If all that is left is a black stone, then surely the one I dropped was the white one. I am innocent." The man was released.[26]

Often things work out for us in ways that take us by surprise. However, later we recognize that God must have been at work in our lives, showing us care and guidance. Sometimes this is called coincidence. But I always say, coincidence is a miracle that God refuses to sign.

God brings us into a land of promise where God inspires us to grow into Christian maturity and wisdom.

And

God brings us into a land of promise where once again God lets us know that God loves us.

I remember hearing Erma Bombeck tell in a television interview of a woman who died of cancer. She wrote notes to her children, telling each that he or she was her favorite and that she loved that child the best because of some particular quality. Then she told them never to tell their brothers and sisters about the note. Maybe God is sending us communiqués telling us how much we are loved. The mauve and purple sunset last evening or the spray of autumn gold in the backyard may be reminders of God's love for you.

When the young daughter of a famous artist was teasingly asked by a reporter which child was her mother's favorite, the girl answered, "She loves Jimmy best because he's the oldest; and she loves Johnny best because he's the youngest; and she loves me best because I'm the only girl." It would be difficult to find a better illustration to more clearly explain God's all-enveloping love for each human being. No matter what is going on in your life right now, no matter how low you have fallen, no matter how blue your soul, or how great and wonderful you feel right now, God loves you best because you are a gift God has wrapped in your name and has given to the world to enjoy.

How many times does God need to let us know how much God loves us and wants us to be people of faith in the world? God began telling the Hebrews some four thousand years ago through a covenantal promise, "I will be your God and you shall be my people." Again and again God stated and restated the promise, giving faithful people opportunity after opportunity to accept God's love and to live for God. God continues to find ways to keep the covenant with those who love the Lord.

18

Rules That Make Life Good

Exodus 20:1–17

When we think of the Ten Commandments, the first thing that comes to mind is usually "Thou shalt not!" We cannot be blamed for this. These godly instructions have been taught as negatives since King David was in diapers. It is easy to picture a stern God, finger pointed downward and shaking at your nose, saying, "Every move you make, every step you take, every bond you break, I'll be watching you." Like Santa Claus, "he knows if you've been bad or good, so be good for goodness' sake!"

Some see God just waiting to catch them doing something wrong. A police cruiser sits in the parking lot of the church I serve. The radar beams extend like a spider web ready to grab the next guilty speeder on Bridge Road. It is too bad we have similar negative images of God and the Ten Commandments.

Q. 18. What are the Ten Commandments?

Many churchgoers can recite most of them. These heaven-inspired rules for life have remained unchanged for thirty-three hundred years. God wants us to learn them by heart, value them as valid and God-given, and live them out twenty-four/seven, not as heavy burdens that keep us from having fun but as rules that make life good.

When the Ten Commandments are seen this way and lived out with this attitude, then it is easy to keep on track and avoid facing the consequences of acting against God. As a result, we find help avoiding self-centeredness. God has given humankind the freedom to say yes or no to these rules that make life good.

In love, God created the cosmos. Even though God has all authority over creation, God chose not to be authoritarian in governing creation. Even though God could control every moment of existence on this planet, God does not work this way. Instead, God chose to saturate creation with a risky, dangerous freedom. Moreover, evil and sin create destruction even when human beings seem to be living faithfully. Freedom resonates at all levels of creation. God allows us the freedom to say yes or no to the rules that make life good. Although God does punish bad choices, how we live our lives is important and has an impact on our own well-being and that of others.

1. Honor God Alone. There is just enough room in a person's heart for one focus of worship. Make it the Lord and Creator of life! I like to picture the human heart as being of a certain size. Its dimensions are just right to house the Holy Spirit of God. When we invite Jesus Christ into our hearts, Christ's Spirit moves in and occupies the aching void until it is filled with divine grace. Maybe you sense that emptiness. And no matter what you have tried to fill it with, nothing has worked. This includes busyness, career, hobbies, money, things, alcohol, pornography, an affair, or hundreds of other potential void fillers that cannot satisfy what only God can fulfill.

There is only enough room for *God* at the center of our hearts. We cannot serve two controlling forces, says the Bible (see Matt. 6:24). There is just not enough room in the human heart to house multiple gods. There is only enough space at the center of our hearts for God. Nothing else will fit and nothing else will satisfy.

2. Honor God as Spirit. Religion can build battlements and high walls. The Spirit of God builds bridges. Sacred symbols are secretive; we have to know the code to understand them. However, the Holy Spirit makes it so that everyone can understand God. Statues are cold and inanimate. The Spirit of Jesus is alive and vibrant. Do not let your loyalty be in religion, symbols, or statues. God is a living, dynamic, expressive, interactive divine Spirit. Keep your loyalty and devotion solidly in God alone.

3. Honor God's Name. This means that we must not trivialize God by saying "God" or "Jesus" in derogatory fashion. Cursing or using God's name frivolously reduces the name of the God of Creation to a silly inconvenience or annoyance. By forcing ourselves to honor God's name, we make a conscious decision to push God toward the center of our life, and it is from the center of our life that God is most dramatically felt. If God is off to one side, only noticed when we are in a jam or for an hour on Sunday morning, we set limits to God's accessibility. What impact can God have on our life from this place?

We must practice centering God back into a key position in our life. We need to work on honoring God's name in our casual conversations, in our humor, our entertainment, and even in our disagreements and moments of anger. As we honor God's name, God will move toward the center.

4. Honor Worship. "Seven days without God makes one weak!" The human psyche is designed by our Creator to find renewal at intervals of seven days. When we read this commandment in the Bible, we will notice that it uses more words than the other commandments. The simple ones are clear: don't lie, don't steal, don't kill. Can it be that, even back then, setting aside time for God took a lot of explaining and convincing? Of all the rules that make life good, this one produces immediate results. Take a break from the workaday world. Rest in the Lord!

5. Honor Parents. In spite of the talk shows that keep telling us that our parents and upbringing are the root of all our troubles, including phobias and low self-esteem, the rules that make life good tell us to *honor* mother and father (or those who took on those roles for us).

It is easy to become parents. And I don't know any parents who look into the eyes of a newborn and say, "How can we screw up this child?" Our parents loved us, maybe only in the most rudimentary way, but love played a part in our coming into the world. Maybe we did not get all the hugs we wanted, but they fed, clothed, and nurtured us so that we are alive today. Mom and Dad maybe even stayed together for the sake of the kids. That's something, isn't it? And children are not always the easiest people to get along with, either! A crying, colicky baby can make even the most loving parent wonder why parenthood sounded so wonderful only a few months ago.

Teenagers, please hear this: Parents are not the enemy. They are your best advocates, and someday you will realize this. It may not seem like it to you, but what they do, they do because they love you and want to protect you, often from the very dangers they experienced at your age. And to my fellow parents, keep one thing in mind. We are bigger than they are and it is *our* house!

6. Honor Life. Work at life-giving endeavors. Work at life-saving causes. Work at life-enriching relationships. Work at life-fulfilling dreams. Work at life-sustaining faith. Work at life-redeeming attitudes. Honor life—every life!

7. Honor Promises of Love. The bond of marriage is second only to the relationship we have with God. Stay true to your mate no matter what the temptations, no matter what the circumstance, no matter how green the grass looks on the other side of the fence. Stay true. Honor your promises of love.

8. Honor What Belongs to Others. Do not steal. Work for what you want. We can steal more than possessions. We can always get another car or wallet, but some things that are stolen can never be restored. We can steal the spotlight. We can steal someone away from another. We can steal the dignity from a person. We can steal ideas. We can steal the dreams and enthusiasm from others by being critical and pessimistic. We can steal the joy of life by not forgiving. We can steal someone's ease by being the office bully.

A number of years ago, when I was the minister of a church in Florida, our church secretary embezzled $13,000 of church funds. She tried to excuse her crime by saying, "The church members have so much and I have so little. I deserve the money." No one owes you a thing, except respect and equal opportunity. This commandment provides clear guidance: Don't steal or take what is not yours, or what you did not earn. Work for what you want. Make sure you deserve it as a reward for hard work and an honest effort.

9. Honor Truth. There are four ways to be guilty of falsehood: to knowingly lie; to distort the facts; to lead someone on with false promises; to tell someone what they want to hear even if it is not completely true. We may be careful not to knowingly lie, but we need to work hard to avoid committing other falsehoods. Honoring the truth is a rule that makes life good.

10. Honor Neighbors. Don't wish to be someone else. Don't wish to be able to do what someone else does well. Don't wish to have the things someone else has. Don't wish to be somewhere else—at a different job, a different city, with a different spouse, with a different boyfriend or girlfriend.

Lottery dreams are empty. You're scratching the wrong itch. Wishes indicate lack of contentment. To be wishing some of the time likely means that you are unhappy at some level. If you are wishing all the time, there is a problem.

Wishes are different from dreams. Dreams lead to plans, and plans lead to hard work, and hard work leads to dreams coming true. Wishes start and finish with the wish itself. Dreams motivate us to grow and change and pray and act differently. Wishes leave us where we are . . . dissatisfied. Dream on! But don't wish too much. Dreams lead to action, wishes to heartache. These are the rules that make life good. God would have us learn them and live them, twenty-four/seven.

19
Hear, O Church . . .
Deuteronomy 6:4-5

It was 1954 and George Docherty was the preacher of the prestigious New York Avenue Presbyterian Church in Washington, D.C., the church of Abraham Lincoln and evangelist Peter Marshall. Among the members of Rev. Docherty's congregation were prominent United States senators and congressmen. Docherty, a naturalized citizen of Scottish birth, expressed in the morning sermon his love for America. He explained how, from his vantage point, he saw the hand of God at work in the history and destiny of his adopted country. His sermon challenged his congregation and those politicians with ears to hear what it would mean to acknowledge God as the prime source of our national values. What would it mean for Americans, whenever they placed a hand over heart to say the "Pledge of Allegiance," not only to pledge their loyalty to the symbol of a great nation, but also to affirm the prime source of our freedoms and dignity? Why not insert the words "under God" between the phrases "one nation" and "indivisible" as a way of honoring our founding principles?

The challenge did not fall on deaf ears. The stirring sermon ignited a groundswell of excitement for the idea of honoring God in the Pledge of Allegiance. The idea made it to the halls of Congress, where a bill was introduced, debated, passed, and signed into law by President Eisenhower in 1954. From that time forth, the sixty-two-year-old Pledge of Allegiance would include the words: "One nation *under God*, indivisible, with liberty and justice for all."

As Americans, we place a hand over our heart and pledge allegiance to the flag, the symbol of the freedom and liberty for which our nation stands. Have you ever wondered what other nations pledge their loyalty to? How about North Korea or Communist China? Their pledge would be very different from ours. When we look down the time line of history, nations and empires like Saddam's Iraq, Nazi Germany, Napoleon's France, the Roman Empire, and Babylon, we might wonder to what or to whom they pledged their loyalty. Did citizens of these nations have the freedom to refuse to pledge? Did they have the option to debate whether it is even right to pledge allegiance, or whether God should be a part of the pledge? The Confessing Church of

Germany in the 1930s was crushed for challenging its nation's ultimate focus of allegiance.

There has only been one nation in history whose pledge of allegiance begins and ends with God. Their pledge is not to a flag or a Führer or a statue of Caesar, but to the Lord and Giver of Life. The youngest children learn this pledge of allegiance and it is often on the lips of those who are breathing their last breath. It is said every day and on holidays and at worship each week. Some say it as they awake in the morning while others say it as they close their eyes before sleep. This pledge is called the *Shema*, and it is the heart of Israel's faith in one God. Jesus recited it as the core meaning of the commandments.

Q. 19. What is the main point of these commandments?

A. 19. You shall love the Lord your God with all your heart, mind, and strength; and you shall love your neighbor as yourself.

The catechism omits the opening remark that every Jewish child can say by heart: "Hear O Israel, the Lord our God is One Lord." The Shema continues with the words: "You shall love the LORD your God with all your heart, and with all your soul, and with all your might" (Deut. 6:4–5). This is the pledge of allegiance that Jesus cited, as did Paul and David and Esther and Ruth and Daniel and Elijah. Jesus cited a second great commandment, from Leviticus 19:18: "You shall love your neighbor as yourself" (Mark 12:31). This summarizes the last six of the Ten Commandments.

These two great commandments form a pledge that the contemporary church needs to say as often as we say the Lord's Prayer, or the Twenty-third Psalm, or the Pledge of Allegiance to the flag of the United States of America.

Our church children learned a cute acronym that I hope helped them understand this pledge of allegiance to God. F.R.O.G. stands for **Fully Rely on God.** It is a modern version of the ancient Hebrew Shema: "Hear, O Church, Fully Rely on God!"

Fully

When we think about pledging to *fully* trust in God, *fully* connotes commitment. A commitment is a twenty-four/seven issue. Twenty-four hours a day, seven days a week, we fully put our life, our dreams, our loved ones, our future in the hands of God in hopes that God will work through us and that we will be worked into God's will.

One evening at a youth rally, the students acted out the story of Telemachus, a man who fully relied on God. Telemachus was a Christian believer who was concerned about the brutality the Roman Empire enjoyed as sport. The Roman Empire had reached a point of depravity by the violence within the Coliseum—gladiators, lions, blood, cheering for more and more violence. Death had turned into entertainment. Children watched and cheered as lions mauled Christians in the arena. Those who killed for sport were heroes one day and lion food the next. Finally, Telemachus could take no more of it. He jumped out of the Coliseum stands, stood in front of the crowd, raised his arms above his head, and said, "In the name of God, stop this madness!" The crowds turned on him, yelling, "Kill him!" They did. However, Telemachus never could have guessed that the Emperor Honorarius would be so disturbed by that incident that in a very short time he would sign an imperial decree that ended the gladiatorial games.

To say to *fully* rely on God sometimes means that it takes our full measure of allegiance to honor God with how we live our lives. We may never face a situation such as the one that Telemachus faced. However, sacrifice may be required whenever we pledge to be God's people in a world that does not understand its own disorder.

Rely

Webster says that "rely" means to depend absolutely on, or to place one's complete confidence in, something or someone. In Israel's pledge of allegiance, that "someone" is God. "Love the LORD with all your heart, soul, and strength" is how Scripture puts it in Deuteronomy 6. But in our day, we are told that we can count on no one but ourselves. But what happens when you cannot even count on yourself, and you let yourself down?

There is an ancient Greek legend about a strong athlete who ran in a famous race. He was sure he was the fastest and no one could beat him. His self-confidence was high, yet he came in second. The town built a statue of the winner, and this made this second-place runner consider himself a loser. It bothered him so much it even became a nightmare that haunted him every night. He could not live without doing something to restore his honor. So at night, he would sneak out to the statue and chisel away at the base of it. Night after night he chipped away at the base, hoping that eventually it would fall and crash to the ground. But one night he went too far. Chiseling the base, he chipped out too much and the statue fell on top of him. He died beneath the crushing weight of the marble statue of the one who reminded him that he was a loser. Placing confidence in himself alone as the solution to his problem, he came to the logical end result, death by his own self-centered plan.

Israel pledged its full confidence not in its armies or songs of worship or even its kings, but in the Lord and Giver of Life. What does this mean for the contemporary church? Are we to do the same?

A young man who had gone off to war in Europe wrote to his father, "I'm sending you all my keys except the front-door key; someday, when I'm on leave, I'll surprise you." When the parents read the letter, they thought, "What a good son. He has no secrets to hide from us, nothing to be embarrassed about, no belongings to be ashamed of. He knows himself and he trusts us. He has given us the run of all his affairs. He has sent us all his keys. He knows us, too. He knows he will always be welcome; that he can always walk in without waiting for us to answer the door. He knows he is always welcome to come home. Our home is open to him and his heart is open to us."

To fully rely on God is to give God all your keys. Have complete confidence in God's grace and judgment. Open your life to him fully and keep nothing back. And you will always have an open door into God's own heart, although our heavenly Father will never be surprised when we visit in prayer.

When Israel pledged allegiance to the Lord, they were giving God all their keys, fully confiding in God's love and grace. They held nothing back, relying fully on God, and God blessed them with divine care and presence.

On God

Imagine a young man proposing to his girlfriend by saying, "Honey, I love you and I want to marry you. I'll do everything in my power to be the best husband ever. I'll be your friend, your confidant, and a great father to our children. All I ask is that you allow me one day a year to set aside my marriage vows and spend time with another woman."

Is there any woman who would accept such an offer? Why do we think God accepts part-time allegiance? There is a reason Israel's pledge of allegiance begins with the command to "hear."

I love the parenting technique I have seen advanced by so many really good moms and dads. A child argues for mom or dad to change a "no" into a "yes." And the parent says, "Child, what part of 'no' don't you understand?" God says, "Hear! O church. Do you get it? Do you really hear me? I am the one and only God in your life, and I expect full-time allegiance. I want your life to be for me."

On March 30, 1981, Ronald Reagan was giving a speech to 3,500 members of the AFL-CIO at the Washington Hilton. John Hinckley, Jr., was waiting outside the hotel with a handgun. When the president came through the doors, Hinckley fired six shots into the presidential entourage, with one bullet ricocheting off a car and hitting Reagan in the chest. Doctors found the bullet only inches from his heart. If it had traveled just a little bit more, it would have killed the president. During Reagan's recovery, Terence Cardinal Cooke of New York City visited and had prayer with the president on Good Friday. Reagan told the cardinal that whatever time he had left would be for God.

Giving your full allegiance to God, as the Shema requires, means F.R.O.G.—to fully rely on God. How does one do that? The best place to start is to look at God's self-revelation to the world. Our pledge of allegiance has us face the Holy Land, where we can see the one who came to show us what God himself is like.

"Hear, O Church, Fully Rely on God."

20

First the Bad News

1 Samuel 3:19–20; Isaiah 9:6–7; Jeremiah 23:5; Deuteronomy 29:25–27

Y‾ou have heard the old saying "I have good news and bad news. Which do you want to hear first?" The next two catechism questions are a "good news, bad news" kind of thing. First we hear the bad news.

Q. 20. Did the people keep their covenant with God?

A. 20. Though some remained faithful, the people too often worshiped other gods and did not love each other as God commanded. They showed us how much we all disobey God's law.

Although God showed the people of Israel wondrous examples of love and grace by giving them the Ten Commandments and a homeland, God 's people continued to go their own way and to ignore God. They did not love one another, and they placed their faith in imitation gods, directly going against God's command to love only the Lord. Because of this, God's anger grew, and God's disappointment swelled for a people that were meant to reveal to the world what God's love was all about. Israel's story shows us how much all of us disobey God's ways, how we have all sinned and fallen short of God's great expectations. We continue to live in a fallen world where nature—as well as social and economic systems—is part of the brokenness of which we are so aware. We may be disappointed and angry, but we should not be surprised when news about corporate corruption like that of Enron, WorldCom, or Adelphia splashes across the front pages of the *Wall Street Journal*. Nor should we be surprised when Imelda Marcos says that all she wants for her birthday is exoneration from corruption charges. We live in a world marked by the Seven Deadly Sins, and a million more just as bad.

Jesus charged us to keep all the commandments of God: Love the Lord with all your heart, mind, soul, and strength and your neighbor as yourself. Yet sin, and the gray fallout cloud that follows it, plagues our world, and the commandments are abandoned along the roadside like a vehicle out of gas. War, unbelief, evil, pain, suffering, disease, prejudice, greed, selfishness, alienation, terrorism, cheating, divorce, addiction, abuse, estrangement—the fallout of our brokenness litters the stories of our lives and the time line of history.

From a distance, we all appear unthreatening, but our sinful nature causes us to strain and stress with one another when we get close. Human nature seems to show its worst side in families, with those whom we love (or should love) the most. Why is it that *brokenness* is so often the caption under the family portrait? The world is skewed and out of plumb. Israel's story shows all of us just how far removed we are from God's great expectations for us. That's the bad news! Now the good news:

Q. 21. What did God do to bring them back to the covenant?

A. 21. Although God judged the people when they sinned, God still loved them and remained faithful to them. God sent them prophets to speak God's word. God gave them priests to make sacrifices for their sins. God called kings to protect the needy and guarantee justice. At last God promised to send the Messiah.

In a much-abbreviated fashion, the selected Scriptures in the heading of the chapter chronicle the sending of priests, kings, prophets, and eventually the Messiah. Each had a message and a mission that corresponded to God's will for the people. The priests offered forgiveness, the kings offered justice, the prophets offered a new word from God, and the Messiah offered lasting salvation. With each godly office—priest, king, prophet, and Messiah—the intention was the same: to call the people to holy living where grace, mercy, love, and second chances are the norm. These are not new concepts for the world. From day one, we have been a people who worship a God of the second chance.

The message is clear, constant, and consistent. Although we so often distance ourselves from God, God keeps finding ways and using people to reconnect us to God's grace and love. This includes that particular means of grace central to the church. In the Lord's Supper, the people of God are once again reminded of holy history and the lengths to which God has gone to bless and redeem the world. If you are sensing that you are distant from God, find God at the Lord's Table on Sunday. If you are in need of reconciliation with someone, find the motivation at the Lord's Table. If you have a prejudice or cannot love your enemy as Jesus commands, find the love to do this at the Lord's Table. And if you need God to save your soul and give you new life, come and eat the bread and drink this cup at the Lord's Table, for it is the cup of salvation and the bread of life for all people.

21

Jesus, Jesus, Jesus . . .

Luke 2:10-11, 22-33; 3:22; 4:16-19

A recent Gallup Poll asked the public this question: "If you could choose a famous person from history, with whom would you like to spend a day?" The most popular response was Jesus. It was even the top choice of those who said they were not Christian believers. It seems that there is just something about Jesus that intrigues even the most skeptical people.

Another poll asked Americans, "In what way has Jesus Christ entered your life or been having an effect on your life?" Seventy-eight percent of respondents said Jesus touched their lives in some way. For instance, Jesus had helped or guided someone. Jesus provided an example to follow. Jesus helped during an illness or health crisis. Jesus helped people to have compassion. Jesus improved the outlook of persons. Jesus made some people better persons. Jesus blessed people with better lives and loving families. Only 22 percent said that they did not know whether Jesus affected their lives or not. That is an amazing statistic. Seventy-eight percent of Americans believe Jesus somehow affects their lives. But many still have trouble believing in Jesus.

An Old Testament proverb says that one of the things the world cannot tolerate is a servant who becomes a king (Prov. 30:21). That is what happened in the case of Jesus. Some have trouble believing that a peasant carpenter from a backwater, hillbilly town in Galilee could possibly be the Son of God, the Savior of the world, and King of the Universe. He never wrote a book, and he never traveled more than one hundred miles from his home. He had no college degree, his followers were fisherman and riffraff, he had no money or home to call his own, and he was ordained into ministry by a rebel who later had his head cut off for insulting the king. He was ratted out by one of his own men, and finally died a criminal's death on a Roman cross. No wonder that Jesus is a stumbling block for some people who would like to believe in God but cannot get past the Jesus thing.

Best-selling author Kathleen Norris, in her book *Amazing Grace*, writes about her own trouble with Jesus. Thinking back to when she first began attending church services as an adult, she found that the language of Jesus, meant to be inviting, made her feel left out. She writes,

Seeking in vain for both signs and wisdom I experienced Jesus only as a stumbling block and foolishness. But that began to change when an unlikely trio—a Pentecostal Baptist woman . . . a Catholic bishop . . . and a Lutheran friend . . . —all happened to thank me for *my love of Christ.* I didn't think I had any, but I began to realize that the joke might be on me.[27]

Jesus was a stumbling block to Norris's belief until it was pointed out to her that Jesus' love was seen in her. Then she started to believe.

As we have worked through the contemporary catechism, we have learned so far that God created the world good and populated it with creatures and human beings to glorify God. But our brokenness caused an estrangement with God, which includes nature and society as a whole. God wanted to restore creation to goodness and so God chose a people. God promised to be their God. He gave them the Ten Commandments to guide them and even a piece of land to call their own. But the people continued to turn away from God, so God sent priests, kings, and prophets to call the people back to their faith and to holy living. Finally, God sent God's own Son to be the Savior of the world.

Q. 22. Who was sent to be the Messiah?

A. 22. God sent Jesus to be the Messiah. Messiah means "anointed one." The New Testament word for Messiah is Christ. Jesus is called the Christ, because God anointed him to be the Savior who would rescue us from sin and death.

What is so cool about this is that the answer is really just another way of expressing John 3:16. **God *sent* his Son to *save*.** In other words: "God so loved the world that he gave his only Son, so that everyone who believes in him may not perish but may have eternal life" (John 3:16).

As we are introduced to Jesus in the next section of the catechism, three words that start with an "S" can help us better understand Jesus: **Sent, Son, and Save.**

God *sent* Jesus to be the Messiah. When we think about someone being sent, it means that someone has authority to do the sending and that someone must make the decision to send. That "someone" is God. Salvation is God-initiated. Theology says it this way. The Primordial Being (God the Father) shows Godself in creation through the Expressive Being (the Logos or the Word, who became human in Jesus of Nazareth.). God reveals Godself through the Logos, Jesus the Christ. *This is God's choice and God's decision.* God is initiating a means of restoration of relationships between Creator and creation, between the Lord and his people. This is something that *God* does. It is not a "do it yourself" project.

At a car repair shop in Arkansas, the mechanic has a sign hanging above the cash register. It reads:

$40 hr. labor rate.
$50 hr. if you watch.
$75 hr. if you help.
$100 hr. if you tried to fix it yourself before you brought it in
for repairs.

Spiritual restoration is not a "fix it yourself" kind of thing. Rather, it is God's way of making things right between us.

God sent Jesus to be the Messiah. Messiah means "anointed one." The New Testament word for Messiah is Christ. In other words, **Jesus is the *Son* of God.**

Prophets or other religious leaders commonly anointed royalty and warrior leaders with oil and ritual prayer as symbol of their new power. Many people were anointed in Old Testament times, and a lot of them could have been called "messiah," which means "anointed one." But over time the messiah was understood to be the Son of God who would come into the world and restore it to God's order. By the intertestamental period (400 B.C. to the time of Christ's birth), an understanding of what and who the Messiah was to be was well-known within Jewish thought. Luke reports a touching story about a man named Simeon who had waited his whole life for the Christ to come. God had set in his heart a craving for the Messiah, but his heart was nearing its last beats and he had yet to find God's Anointed One who would save the world.

"Just one more day, Simeon," the Holy Spirit said. "Just one more trip to the Temple, faithful servant—trust me!" Simeon took the baby in his arms and lifted him toward heaven and blessed him. Mary and Joseph did not quite understand, but Simeon knew that the Messiah had come.

The word "Messiah" or "Christ" became such a politically charged word in the early days of the church that the Christians avoided it out of fear for their lives. For a time they used a code to identify themselves as followers of Jesus, the Christ. The word "fish" in Greek (*ichthus*), or the symbol of a fish, secretly announced that a person was a Christian: *Iesous Christos Theou Huios Soter*—**Jesus Christ—God's Son—Savior.**

The acronym **ICHTHUS** shows development of the New Testament meaning of the word messiah, the anointed one (*Christos*). Jesus is the Anointed One, the promised Christ who is God's Son, the Expressive Being of the Trinity, and has come to restore all creation to the Creator, to make right our relationship with our God.

God sent Jesus to *save*. Messiah means "anointed one." The New Testament word for Messiah is Christ. Jesus is called the Christ because God anointed him to be the Savior who would rescue—or *save*—us from sin and death.

The name "Jesus" is the Greek form of a Hebrew name. The Hebrew is Joshua or Yehoshuah, which means "Yahweh is salvation," or "God saves."

Jesus' very name defines his heavenly mission to earth. On behalf of God he saves us and restores us to a right relationship with our God. In C. S.

Lewis's science fiction *Space Trilogy,* the main character is a Christ figure named Dr. Ransom. Lewis plays with the name of this interstellar traveler in much the same way as the Bible uses the name Jesus as a hidden way to explain his life and death. Ransom is another way of expressing "rescued" or "saved." Ransom is one English translation of Yehoshuah, Jesus.

The contemporary catechism puts it this way: God made Jesus to be the Savior who would rescue us from sin and death. It could easily have read: "who would ransom or save us from our brokenness." God could have used just one word to say it all: JESUS, JESUS, JESUS. Jesus came to take upon himself the sins of the world.

Sid Fleischman's Newbery medal–winning book *The Whipping Boy* begins with an episode that explains what a whipping boy is. The young prince was known here and there as *Prince Brat.* Not even black cats would cross his path. One night the king was holding a feast. Sneaking around behind the guests, Prince Brat tied their powdered wigs to the backs of their chairs and hid behind a footman to wait for the action. When the guests stood up to toast the king, their wigs flew off. The lords gripped their bare heads as if they'd been scalped. The ladies shrieked in horror. Prince Brat tried to keep from laughing. He clapped his hands over his mouth but out came laughter.

The angry king saw him. He gave a furious shout. "Fetch the whipping boy!" Prince Brat knew that he had nothing to fear. He never felt a whipping in his life. He was a prince, after all, and it was forbidden to spank a prince. A common boy was kept in the castle to be punished in his place. "Fetch the whipping boy!" An orphan named Jemmy, the son of a rat catcher, awakened. "Ain't I already been whipped twice today? What's the prince done now?" The king gave the order for twenty stripes. Biting back every cry, the whipping boy received the twenty whacks. The king turned to the prince and said, "And let that be a lesson to you!"[28]

The Whipping Boy is Jesus. He takes upon himself what is due you and me, and this is the means of grace that God has established to rescue us from sin and death.

There is a story about the renowned theologian and exile from Nazi Germany Karl Barth. When he visited Union Seminary in Richmond, a faculty member asked him what he would say to Adolf Hitler if he met him face to face. Professor Barth's reply was, "Jesus Christ died for your sins." How simplistic. How irrelevant and how utterly absurd seemed his reply to the pragmatic ears of American theologians! But many suspect that it was Barth's way of saying to his listeners, in the context of a brief conversation, that in the end, the church has only one message—Jesus Christ saves us from sin and death.

SENT—SON—SAVE: three basic things we need to know about JESUS.

22
INCLUSIONIS!
Galatians 3:6–7

If Jesus were a wizard like Harry Potter, the magic spell he would cast would sound like this: *In-clu-si-on-is!*

He would be performing something that theologians include under the rubric of *soteriology*. As we look at what the contemporary catechism teaches us about Jesus, it is important for us to know this term and another, *christology*. The catechism deals with both of these two theological doctrines.

Christology is the study of the person and the work of Jesus Christ. Who he was, what he did during his lifetime, the titles the Bible gives him, his ministry, and the content of his preaching are all included in Christology. Albert Schweitzer's famous *The Quest of the Historical Jesus* (1910) is an example of Christology.

Soteriology is the study of the work of Christ, but with the lens focused specifically on what Jesus accomplished through his life, death, and resurrection for the salvation of the world. *Inclusionis!* is a soteriological issue. It refers to what Jesus' death accomplished in terms of the covenant promises of the Old Testament.

Q. 23. How did God keep the promise to Abraham by sending Jesus?

A. 23. By sending Jesus, God opened up the covenant with Abraham to the whole world. God welcomed all who have faith in Jesus into the blessings of the covenant.

Inclusionis! is the word that opens up the promises of God, not only to the Jews, but also to anyone, Jew or Gentile, who has faith in Jesus Christ. God welcomes into the family of faith those who believe.

Of course, *Inclusionis!* has no inherent power in itself. Go ahead and say it. See, nothing happens! It is the fact that Jesus says it that makes it a powerful word.

Some people, such as Rev. Sun Myung Moon, think that the work of Christ for salvation was incomplete. They are wrong! The work of Christ is all God needed to open the door to a new, God-centered life for all who believe in him. But we have to respond to God's initiative.

I was so happy when spell-checkers for computers were introduced. I am the world's worst speller. For the longest time, I had to keep looking up how to spell my middle name, Michael. No kidding! Things like that just don't stick in my brain. Spell-checking was a divine answer to prayer. When I finished my first sermon on my first computer that came equipped with spell-checker, I clicked on the spell-checker icon. The program stopped at the word "Jesus" with the comment "Does not exist." I had to insert Jesus into the computer's vocabulary.

In the same way, Jesus does not exist in anyone's vocabulary until they intentionally insert it into the vocabulary of their life. The work of Christ makes this a possibility. This is what Christians call salvation.

Frederick Buechner says salvation is more of an experience than a doctrine. Salvation is losing yourself and finding that you are more fully yourself than usual. It's like love.

> When you love somebody, it is no longer yourself who is the center of your own universe. It is the one you love who is. You forget yourself. You deny yourself. You give of yourself so that by all the rules of arithmetical logic there should be less of yourself than there was to start with. Only by a curious paradox there is more. You feel that at last you really are yourself.[29]

He says that the experience of salvation involves the same paradox. Jesus puts it thus: "Those who lose their life for my sake will find it" (Matt. 10:39). Salvation is living for the one who holds your heart in his gentle, loving hands.

And it can happen anytime. You may remember in the movie *Field of Dreams* when the old-time baseball players mysteriously walk out of the cornfield. All the greats of baseball history are there. Shoeless Joe Jackson says that all the players wanted to come to play, even Ty Cobb, but he was such an SOB that they told him "No."

Although Cobb's accomplishments on the field were legendary, he was said to be the meanest and most unlikable man who ever played the sport. Yet on his deathbed on July 17, 1961, he accepted Jesus Christ as his Savior. He said, "You tell the boys I'm sorry it was the last part of the ninth that I came to know Christ. I wish it had taken place in the first half of the first."[30]

Inclusionis! is a word for all persons. From our standpoint, we may wonder whether a particular person knows the grace and love of God and if they are included in the work of Jesus on the cross. Yet the Christian faith insists that God welcomes anyone who believes to share the blessings of the covenant.

Nicky Gumbel, an Anglican minister from England and teaching minister for the popular Alpha Course, a practical introduction to the Christian faith, tells a story about his father. Nicky became a Christian shortly before his father died. He was practicing law at the time and as a newer believer wondered if his father, who was not a churchgoing man, was at peace with God. Ten days after his death, he was reading his Bible in hopes of finding an answer. He happened to be reading Romans 10 and came across this sentence: "Everyone who calls on the name of the Lord shall be saved" (Rom. 10:13). He sensed that God was trying to tell him something important in this verse about his father. About five minutes later his wife came into the room and said she had been reading a verse that seemed to be directed to his question about his father. His wife said, "I think this verse is for your father. It's from Acts 2:21: "Then everyone who calls on the name of the Lord shall be saved." It was extraordinary because that verse appears only two times in the New Testament and God had spoken them both at the same time!

Three days later, he went to a Bible study at a friend's home and the topic was Romans 10:13: "Everyone who calls on the name of the Lord shall be saved." Nevertheless, he was still thinking about his father and wondering about his eternal fate. On the way to work, he was getting off the subway and saw a large billboard on which the words "Everyone who calls on the name of the Lord will be saved" were written. He talked to the pastor at his church and his minister said, "Do you think the Lord may be trying to tell you something?"[31]

We don't know what a person prays or says to God. All we know is that Jesus offers a divinely inspired word to everyone, *Inclusionis!* It is a fancy way of saying, "You are included in the work of Jesus Christ for salvation." God is at work in Christ to rescue the world from its brokenness. Sometimes we may not be able to see the work of Christ, as our salvation is being played out behind the scenes. But pay attention—the work of Christ for salvation continues to transform all who believe. His word today is *Inclusionis!* You are included in his work on the cross.

23

Was Jesus Just Another Human Being?

Matthew 1:22-23; John 1:1, 14; Colossians 1:15, 19-20

A minister in a Kentucky church wanted to talk to the children about Noah's ark during worship. She came up with a brief game in which the children would identify animals that Noah would have brought onto the ark. She told the children, "I am going to describe something to you. Let's see if you can guess what it is. First, it has a bushy tail and is furry. It climbs trees, eats nuts, and is usually gray, but it can be red or black or brown. Its favorite food is acorns. What am I describing?" The children were silent, looking as if the minister had asked them about quantum physics. She said, "Do you know what I am describing?" There was silence. She turned to the little girl who always had an answer and asked, 'Michelle, what do you think?" Michelle looked hesitantly at the other children and said, "Well, I know the answer has to be Jesus, but it sure sounds like a squirrel to me!"

Q. 24. Was Jesus just another human being?

Our hesitant response can easily be, "No, but he sure looks like one to me." Our first impression is correct. You might say to yourself, "No, he wasn't just another human being, but everything about him makes it sound like he was." The facts show that he was born of a woman. He had all the needs and made all the demands infants and toddlers make upon their parents. He had to learn to walk, may have sucked his thumb, probably argued with his younger brothers and sisters. He fell down and hurt himself, he had to learn to read and write, he probably hit his thumb with a hammer in the carpenter's shop. He dealt with the issues of adolescence, was tempted to do things God would not have approved, and probably had his heart broken. He got angry, laughed, danced, drank, ate, slept, sweated, wept, bled, and died. He sure sounds like just another human being to me!

But "No" is the correct answer.

A. 24. Although he was truly human, he was God with us. As someone who was truly human, he could share all our sorrows. Yet because he was truly God, he could save us from all our sins.

Jesus was a human being who walked the earth some two thousand years ago. We are assured there is historical proof other than the Gospels of his life, teaching, arrest, execution, and burial. Jesus really was a human being on this earth, born, living and dying. Historians, including the chronicler of the first century Judaism, Josephus, tell us that there was a human being named Jesus. But Jesus must have been more than just another ordinary human being. If he had been just a great teacher, philosopher, or radical religious rabbi, the world might have been a better place thanks to his teachings, but he could not have transformed lives as he did when his name was invoked in prayer. There must be something more to Jesus of Nazareth.

The apostle Paul tried to explain it to the Christians living in Colossae, a town in what is now Turkey. He said that Jesus is the image of the invisible God. In Jesus the essence of God is present. Jesus expresses God's love and grace for the world. The Lord of the universe is our Lord and Savior. Jesus the man is at the same time the essence of God. When we see Jesus in the Gospel stories, we see God in action. The powerful proclamation of Emmanuel declares that God is with us in Christ (Matt. 1:23).

What do I believe? Is Jesus just another human being, or is Jesus in fact God present with us then and now? All I can say is that a philosophy of a first-century rabbi would have no power to transform my life and redeem my soul. The teachings of a mere man who lived two thousand years ago could in no way be revealed through the way my life was transformed from lost-ness to one that looked to a bright future. All I can say is that if Jesus had been just another human being, I would not be here today telling you that I believe he is the Lord of life and my eternal friend. If Jesus were just another person, I would be just one more broken, unhappy human being living a miserable, meaningless existence. Let me explain the twisted tale of how Jesus supernaturally transformed my life and directed me according to God's will so that I would be at this keyboard writing about my faith.

When I was twenty years old, my life was dry, empty, and at a standstill. I grew up in the church, but as a teenager I stopped attending and stopped believing. I completely forgot about God and was concerned only with myself. By age twenty, I had seven years under my belt of underage drinking, smoking dope, and, like many of my friends, experimenting with harder drugs, such as LSD and speed. By the time I reached age twenty, my circle of high school friends had disappeared, with the exception of my girlfriend. She was the only one whom I could continue to trust. In high school and college, I existed for one purpose: to find some kind of manufactured thrill that would prove I was alive. My girlfriend is now my wife. She once said, "If I had been your mother, I would have grounded you forever!"

By age twenty, I had come to an unemotional standstill; my life seemed to be a dry, empty nothing. My father had a future planned for me as a foreman in the local Nabisco plant, and I guess I would have gone that route: a training program at the Milk Bone plant in Buffalo and then on to supervise a department in a Nabisco plant making Shredded Wheat or Oreo cookies. He had signed me up to go. But then I met Al.

First, some background. It is amazing how life can wind itself into granny knots and still make sense. God's wisdom, will, and providence are often illustrated by the metaphor of an elaborate tapestry. From the back the tapestry is just a tangle of multicolored threads without rhyme or reason, but when one turns it over and looks at it from the front, it is a wonderful work of art.

Sunday school teacher Edward Kimball could not have imagined that his humble efforts to teach some young adults about Jesus would make that much difference in the world. Kimball was not even sure if his teaching was at all effective. In 1858, he shared his belief in Jesus with a young man who worked as a shoe store clerk. That conversation opened the door for the shoe store clerk to become a Christian. The young man's name was Dwight L. Moody. Years later, Moody became a world-renowned evangelist. A local pastor heard him preach in 1879 at a church meeting in New England, and it sparked a renewal of his own faith. The local pastor's name was F. B. Meyer.

Thanks to this new sense of spiritual energy, Pastor Meyer began to lead services at a nearby college. In one of those services, a student's heart was touched by the message, and he opened his life to the touch of God's love. He became a believer and offered his life to Jesus to do with it as Jesus pleased. The student's name was J. Wilbur Chapman. Chapman later worked for the YMCA. The YMCA was one of the most effective organizations of its day for the purpose of sharing the gospel with young people. It hosted revival meetings aimed at teens all across the nation. As the program grew, Chapman hired a Presbyterian evangelist who used to be a baseball player, thinking that the ex–sports star would draw the interest of teenage boys and young men. The young Presbyterian minister was Billy Sunday.

Billy Sunday, like Moody, became the most popular and effective evangelist of his day. After a Billy Sunday revival meeting in Charlotte, North Carolina, a group of young businessmen became so excited about Jesus that they arranged for another series of revivals in Charlotte. This time they invited another popular preacher, Mordecai Ham, to be the speaker. Mordecai Ham preached that Jesus was fully human yet fully God. He preached that lives are changed when Jesus touches them. He preached the truths of the gospel in his services, and a young man from North Carolina came forward to the altar and turned his life over to Christ. The young man who came forward that night was Billy Graham. Billy Graham, like Moody and Sunday, became the most popular and effective evangelist of the second half of the twentieth century. Globe-trotting with the gospel, Graham has preached Christ on every continent except Antarctica. His preaching has been televised and now even his classic television programs are being replayed for a new audience and generation.

In the early 1970s, Billy Graham held a crusade in Buffalo, New York. A twenty-year-old attended one of the meetings. This fledgling Christian heard Graham's call to share the gospel with those whose lives seemed empty and at a dead end. The man who attended that crusade and took to heart the challenge to tell others about Jesus was named Al. Shortly afterward, Al asked a twenty-year-old coworker on the factory floor of the Shredded Wheat plant in Niagara Falls if he wanted his dry, empty, purposeless life to be filled with love and grace and hope. I said, "Yes."

We see the back of "the tapestry" dimly, but someday we will see it from the front and we will marvel at the beauty of its Artist. (See 1 Cor. 13:12.) Edward Kimball never could have imagined that as a result of his Sunday school class, a young man would develop into the world's most popular evangelist. Nor could Wilbur Chapman ever imagine that the former baseball player he hired, whose trademark was "Slide into heaven," would preach a sermon that would start in motion a series of events that someday would allow the gospel to be broadcast to every corner of the globe. Billy Graham had no idea that Al was one of the fifty thousand in the stadium that night, nor that Al would follow through on the challenge to share the gospel with a hurting friend. Yet through a string of events, Jesus artfully worked his divine will and offers evidence that he is not just another human being, but is in deed God with us, our Emmanuel.

24
What Was Jesus Like?
Mark 1:27; Luke 15:4–7; Matthew 11:28–30

Today's Catechism question and answer, and the three readings for today, Mark 1:27, Luke 15:4–7, and Matthew 11:28–30, challenge us to find what they have in common. One good answer is Christology, the theological study of the person and teachings of Jesus Christ. Our three texts help us to understand what Jesus was like.

Q. 25. What was Jesus like?

A. 25. When Jesus spoke, he spoke with God's authority. When he acted, he acted with God's power. The people were amazed. He was also gentle and loving. He cared for us in all our needs as a shepherd cares for the sheep.

In Mark 1:27 Jesus spoke and acted with the authority of God. The people were amazed and seemed to find Jesus' teaching awesome. "Amazing" and "awesome" are two words that come to mind in this Gospel to describe Jesus' teaching and actions. It's interesting that a favorite hymn of many Americans who grew up in the second half of the twentieth century, "Amazing Grace," and a new favorite hymn of the twenty-first century, "Awesome God," use these same adjectives. These two hymns represent respectively anthems of the over-forty generation and of Generation X, the "twenty-somethings."

What was Jesus like? *Amazing and awesome!* Jesus is still acting in ways that are awesome, and the lessons he passes on to us through Scripture and sermon are still amazing.

A pastor got word from the parents of a college student that she was dropping out of college because of church! They asked the pastor to speak with their daughter to try to talk her out of throwing away all those credits she worked so hard to accumulate. The girl and pastor talked, and she explained that his sermon the day before had started her thinking. He had said that God has something important for each of us to do. She had thought, "I'm not in college because I want to serve God. I am here to get a job, to make money, to look out for myself."

Then she had remembered the summer spent working with migrant workers on behalf of the church. She had felt then that she was really serving

God. So she had decided to drop out of college and give her life to working with these children.

There was a long pause and finally her pastor said, "Now look, I was only preaching!"

Jesus is still working in awesome ways, and the lessons he is teaching are amazing. He will use us to get his work done, whether we are "just preaching" or really mean it. Awesome and amazing is Jesus!

Jesus said, "For I am gentle and humble in heart, and you will find rest for your souls in me" (Matt. 11:29, paraphr.). Jesus was gentle and loving. Now these qualities are purposely juxtaposed to the qualities of awesome and amazing. If Jesus were only gentle and loving, he would be a namby-pamby. If Jesus were only amazingly powerful, he would be an iron-fisted tyrant. Some want Jesus to be a nonviolent peace activist. Others would rather paint their picture of Jesus as a stern schoolteacher, ruler in hand, ready to rap knuckles at the first sign of a broken rule. But Jesus our Lord is *both* loving and powerful, gentle and just, loving us yet challenging us to show the amazing grace that counts others more important than self. This balance of love and power, grace and justice, mercy and selflessness, embrace and challenge reminds me of the description of Aslan, the Lion in C. S. Lewis's children's tale *The Lion, the Witch and the Wardrobe*. When the Lion (who represents Christ in Lewis's magical world) appears to be warm and cuddly, the children are reminded that he is a wild Lion. When the fierce Lion roars, they are reminded that he is a Comforter and Companion.[32] The church that is always actively reforming is a church that balances the gracious embrace of a loving Lord and the challenge to be a people who make a difference in the world in light of God's justice.

In our third passage, Jesus cares for us in all our needs, just as a shepherd cares for his sheep. In Luke 15:4–6, the Good Shepherd leaves the ninety-nine sheep to search for the one lost lamb. Does this sound extreme? Some of us do crazy things to retrieve what we lose. Ron, a member of my church, went looking for his sixteen-year-old, deaf and blind dog last week and fell into the swamp behind his house in the rescue effort. Last week I went to retrieve a golf ball I hit into a sun-dried pond and sank up to my knees in muck.

A decade ago, people shelled out big bucks to own pot-bellied pigs, those exotic house pets from Vietnam. The breeders claimed that they could be housebroken and that they would grow to about 40 pounds. The pigs were smart but they did not grow to 40 pounds. Rather, they regularly grew to over 150 pounds and often became aggressive.

Someone had given Dale a pot-bellied pig. The pig was never housebroken, and he ate the carpet, wallpaper, and drywall under it. Yet Dale loved his pig. He sold his suburban home and moved to the country and built a large pen for his pig. He started taking in unwanted pot-bellied pigs, and before long he was living in hog heaven! He currently has over 180 pigs. They sleep on pine shavings, soak in a plastic swimming pool, and listen to piped-in classical music. They will never fear the butcher. There is a waiting list to get into

Dale's farm. Dale told reporters that he felt we are all put on earth for a particular reason and that he had concluded that pigs were his calling. How could anyone in his right mind fall in love with pot-bellied pigs?

I will tell you something even more amazing. An infinite, perfectly holy, majestic, awesome God is passionately in love with insignificant, broken, self-centered, sometimes openly hostile and frequently indifferent people. God loves people like you and me.

These three texts help us to learn something about the person and teaching of Jesus. All three enhance our understanding of Christology. Together they show us what Jesus was like. When Jesus spoke, he spoke with God's authority. When he acted, he acted with God's power. Yet he was gentle and loving and cared for us in all our needs as a shepherd cares for the sheep.

25

What Did Jesus Do?

Mark 6:41–42; Luke 5:13, 20; Matthew 6:25–34

I t's easy to write a job description. As a minister and head of staff, I have to do that often for both volunteers and paid staff. But it is another thing to find the right worker to fill it. A large corporation listed an opening and position description for a senior vice president. The hiring committee came back with a recommendation that they hire a golden retriever. Their memo read: "His ability to get along with anyone, his eagerness to please humans, his instinct to retrieve what others toss away, his prompt response to a pat on the back, his interest in watching others work, and his great knack for looking wise while saying nothing make him a natural for this position."

Once a year, we celebrate Labor Day and the workers who faithfully fulfill their job descriptions. Once a year is not enough, and the church needs to find ways to celebrate the contribution of all who work for a living. As Presbyterian Christians, we are also challenged to see how what we do to make a living can be seen as a calling from God and an opportunity to be in ministry in the workplace, marketplace, or home.

Question 26 asks us to consider Jesus' job description.

Q. 26. What did Jesus do during his life on earth?

A. 26. He called disciples to follow him. He fed the hungry, healed the sick, blessed children, befriended outcasts, required people to repent, and forgave their sins. He taught people not to fear, but to trust always in God. He preached the good news of God's love and gave everyone hope for new life.

He did all these things and more. And because he did them, he wants us to do them, too. What Jesus did during his life on earth forms a ten-point Job Description for Contemporary Christians as we take up the challenge as his disciples.

There is a story about a statue of Jesus in a square at the center of a city in postwar Europe. The statue was marred from bombing raids. The hands and arms were broken off; the legs were battered, with large fragments of marble missing. The eyes and mouth and ears were damaged from the blasts that leveled the town. The city officials wanted to demolish the statue and erect a new one, but a local pastor protested, saying, "The statue reminds us of what Jesus wants us to do for him. We can be his hands and arms. We can be his feet. We can be his eyes, ears, and mouth to those who need him the most." The statue was kept as it was as a daily reminder of the job description that Jesus' own life on earth sets forth for contemporary Christians.

First, **Jesus called disciples to follow him.** That is what we are to do, too. Invite others to live for Christ. At the church I serve, our Evangelism and Congregational Care Committees are working to enhance our new member orientation so that those who are drawn to our congregation will better be able to live for Christ as his disciples in the matrix of this particular church. If there are folks looking for a new opportunity to serve Jesus Christ, if someone senses a desire to devote one's life to him, if someone is hearing an invitation from the Lord to "follow me," I hope to invite them to prayerfully consider attending the next new member orientation in which they will be challenged to follow the Lord.

Second, **Jesus fed the hungry.** At St. Andrew Church, the challenge to feed the hungry is taken seriously. A Joyful Noise Offering pays for the food the church serves at the monthly Soup Kitchen. The coins add up and surprisingly total an amount that lets the church provide a full meal to over one hundred persons each month.

A Reverse Offering, where worshipers take a brief shopping list from the offering plate and return those items the following Sunday, provides over 80 percent of the food for the local Food Pantry housed at a neighboring church, and the leftovers go to the homeless shelter. Members deliver Meals on Wheels, the Vacation Bible School surpassed its goal to buy bee kits for farmers in developing nations, and on and on the list goes.

Third, **Jesus healed the sick.** Our church is blessed with some of the area's finest doctors, nurses, and health care workers. I am quite impressed at the way their faith flows through their professional work. Irene works in the chaplain's office at a local hospital, helping to provide spiritual care to the sick. Our physicians write prescriptions for prayer, knowing that Jesus, the Great Physician, is always the source of healing. One member surely prays often as he pilots the Nightingale helicopter from a crash site to the hospital. Our Care and Kindness Ministry offers prayer at the bedside of members who are hospitalized. The church is challenged to do what Jesus did—heal the sick.

Fourth, **Jesus blessed the children.** He included them at a time when society treated children as pieces of property, or worse. Children were property that could be used, abused, and thrown away. One of the highlights of the new sanctuary at my church is the Children's Wall and stained glass window depicting the Gospel account of Jesus blessing the children. The motivation for the wall and window was to keep in the forefront of our congregational the reminder that children make up about one-third of our congregation. Even though their voices are heard loud and clear in the hallways and playground, the wall and window allow their voices to be heard among the adult leadership. Recently the elders added a youth elder and a youth deacon to our organizational setup so that the adults could listen to the needs of teenagers in the congregation. We are to always include the needs and contributions of the children in what we do as a church.

Fifth, **Jesus befriended the outcasts.** You and I are called to do the same thing. Hard? Yes. Impossible? No. Can the church help? Yes.

I miss Vern. He was the best at this endeavor. When he served as host at the Soup Kitchen, he would call the regulars by name, hug them, smile, tell jokes, but most of all, show the love of Jesus to everyone no matter what they wore, or how they talked, or how dirty their hands and hair were. He was Jesus' smile for them. He mentored us all in the way Christians can befriend those on the margins of life.

Sixth, **Jesus required people to repent of sinful behavior.** It would make sense that as his faithful disciples, we face a difficult responsibility in challenging persons, institutions, and society to "do the right thing." We bemoan corporate greed but enjoy the profits made when we are involved in deals that shade the truth. We complain about unfair practices but keep quiet when they benefit our position. We regret the hurt caused by gossip, but we listen anyway without cutting off the one telling the tales.

Jesus challenged bad behavior and unjust policies. He refused to listen to excuses that justify prejudice, bigotry, cheating, unfaithfulness, and other individual and corporate sins. One of the hardest things we are asked to do as Christians is to challenge behavior and attitudes that do not honor God. If we don't, who will?

A poster hanging in one of the adult classrooms of the church I serve presents a troubling confession by Pastor Martin Niemöller, speaking for the church after the dark night of the Nazi regime: "First they came for the socialists, and I did not speak out because I was not a socialist. Then they came for the trade unionists, and I did not speak out because I was not a trade unionist. Then they came for the Jews, and I did not speak out because I was not a Jew. Then they came for me, and there was no one left to speak for me."[33] If we don't challenge evil in society and culture, who will?

Seventh, **Jesus forgave sinners.** In the Lord's Prayer, Jesus offered a petition to God and instructed us to "forgive those who sin against us." Just as Jesus forgave sin, we are to forgive those who sin against us. It is the Christian thing to do.

Eighth, **Jesus taught people not to fear.** Jesus' gospel wasn't a "turn or burn" message, although he did indicate that hellish consequences face those who refuse to acknowledge God. The Gospels give example after example of God's goodness and unbelievable grace. They invite us to trust God with heart, mind, soul, and strength. This is the gospel expressed in the contemporary catechism. Our denominational church school material focuses on the goodness and grace of God found in Jesus Christ made known to us through the Holy Spirit. It is an uplifting and faith-building message.

Ninth, **Jesus preached the good news of God's love.** Each August, we have what I call Laity Sunday. On this day, members of our congregation share in word and song a testimony of how God has touched their lives. This is also what I do each week as worship leader. Gospel—*evangelion* in the original New Testament Greek—means the good news and refers to God's love. Find ways to talk about how God has been active in your life. Talk with your children about the moments when you felt close to God, or when God was there for you in a troubling time. Read Bible stories and devotions at home. Look for all the ways that nature's beauty can teach us about God. It is a great way to talk about how God can be seen in nature.

Finally, **Jesus expressed hope.** That's our job, too. We have a great opportunity to offer hope to our friends. The church is the perfect place to foster hope. After a difficult year, our church planned and hosted a community service of remembrance on the anniversary of September 11. It was a dramatically moving experience. People were hungry for hope, and the service offered it in the form of Scripture, prayers, and community building. The service provided closure to a difficult year. People are still worried and frightened for loved ones and their children, and the impact of 9/11 will linger for some time. The evening news offers little hope, but we know where we can turn for a genuine word of hope—Jesus. Let your friends know that your hope is in nothing less than Jesus and his faithfulness.

This is our ten-point job description as believers. What Jesus did in his earthly life provides a blueprint for all of us. Like all real work, it is not going to be easy. If it were easy, we would not call it work! But we find strength for the journey in the company of believers and at the Table of the Lord. Be filled with Christ and then take on the world in his name!

26
Jesus Is Savior and Lord
Luke 22:44–49; 2 Corinthians 5:19

The contestants on *Wheel of Fortune* always get excited when the puzzle has an ampersand in it. Not being the sharpest tool in the shed, I turned to my wife, Debbie, the first time I heard Pat Sajak tell Vanna White to turn the ampersand, and I asked, "What in the world is an ampersand?" She enjoys it when the king of Trivial Pursuit has to ask her about something, especially something as simple as an ampersand. So she made it sound as if everyone knows what an ampersand is. "It's that funny squiggle S-shape that means 'and.' " Curious, I looked it up in my dictionary, which provided about as good an explanation as my wife's. It is the sign for "and" (&), and it stands for "and per se and," meaning that the sign by itself means "and."

Why am I telling you this? Our contemporary catechism, *Belonging to God*, has two questions that go together and almost sound alike. The answers are so similar that I am sure that if the catechism were not written for young children, it would have been combined with the next one. All they would have needed was the addition of an ampersand. So I will do it for them.

Q. 27 & 28. How did Jesus Christ prove to be our Savior & how do we know that Jesus is Lord?

The answers blend together, giving us a powerful testimony of the work of the cross and the power of the resurrection:

A. 27 & 28. Jesus sacrificed his life for us by dying on the cross. He showed his victory over death by rising from the dead. He removed our guilt and gave us new, unending life with God & after he died and was raised from the dead, he appeared to his disciples, both women and men. He revealed himself to them as our living Lord and Savior. Through the Bible, he continues to reveal himself to us today.

The catechism lays the claim that Jesus is Savior & Lord right in our laps. These two biblical terms are conjoined at the hip whenever we use them to refer to Jesus of Nazareth. So it makes perfect sense that a question about Jesus as Lord comes right on the heels of the question of his being our Savior. In fact, we cannot talk about Jesus unless we talk about him as Savior & Lord, together.

The good news of Christianity is that God loves us and did not leave us in the mess we made for ourselves. If we were honest with ourselves, we would admit that we do things that we know are wrong. We discover this passage in an ancient document written to early Christians in Rome: "All of us have sinned and no matter how hard we try, we just don't measure up to the level of excellence that God wants from us" (Rom. 3:23, paraphr.). If we compare ourselves with bank robbers or kidnappers or mobsters, we could say we look pretty good. But when we compare ourselves with Jesus of Nazareth, we see how far short we fall. If we ever took the time to write down our most private thoughts and attitudes, I'm sure we would soon discover that we are filled with sinister thoughts we would just as well not know about. The problem of sin is something we all need to deal with. God came up with a way. God took upon his own shoulders the penalty and saved us from bearing that heavy burden on our frail shoulders.

I got to know Ernest Gordon through a brief correspondence after his retirement from the chapel of Princeton University. He wrote a letter commending me for an editorial I had written in a church magazine, and I enjoyed the brief flurry of notes passed back and forth. Ernest Gordon is the author of *Miracle on the River Kwai*, on which the movie *The Bridge on the River Kwai* and the newer and more accurate movie retelling, *To End All Wars*, were based. One disturbing scene in the movie may help us better understand how God offered a self-substitution for our offenses.

A group of prisoners of war were working on the Burma Railway during World War II. At the end of each day, the tools were routinely collected and counted by their Japanese captors. After a day's work, and the routine gathering and counting of the tools, a shovel was found to be missing. The guards demanded to know which man had taken it. One of the guards began to shout and scream. He ordered the guilty man to step forward. No one moved. "All die! All die!" he yelled, cocking his rifle and aiming it at the prisoners. Then, one man stepped forward, and the guard clubbed him to death with the butt of the rifle. After they returned to the camp, the tools were counted again and this time, all of them were accounted for. They had miscounted and no shovel was missing. That man had stepped forward as a substitute to save the others from certain death.

Jesus, God's beloved Son, stepped forward to take on the deadly penalty for our offenses. Paul wrote, "In Christ, God was reconciling (rescuing or ransoming) the world to himself, not counting their sins against them" (2 Cor. 5:19, paraphr.).

The best image I have of God's love is that of the loving father, running down a dirt road, tunic flowing in the wind, arms wide open as he sees his estranged son making his way back home. The father does not ask his son to pay back the money he blew on fast women and even faster living. Instead the father absorbs the losses himself, counting it more valuable to regain his son (Luke 15). Jesus, God's presence and power in human form, took on a burden the weight of which we could never survive if we were to attempt it on our own. Leave it to God to beat death by giving a life. When we say Jesus is our Savior, we are saying that he saved us from the mess we got ourselves into.

When we call him Lord, it means we look to him as we look to God. Years before, Paul wrote his first letter addressing Jesus as Lord. The believers already had a primitive question-and-answer catechism, but it had only one question: Who is Jesus? Answer: Jesus is Lord. This was the first official creed. It articulated more than just a title of honor or social rank—it professed a theological statement. The New Testament Greek word for "lord" (*kurios*) stands for a variety of Hebrew words for "lord." *Adon* was the basic Hebrew word for Lord, meaning someone in authority or high social rank. In a religious context, "Lord" is a title we give to God Almighty in prayer and song, as in Psalm 150: "Praise the LORD!"

But when we say "Lord" we are also saying the unspeakable name of God, the name God whispered to Moses from a bush that burned but was not consumed by the flames. The Tetragrammaton (YHWH) is the name God gave to Moses. When the special name of God was withdrawn from public use by the rabbis so that it would not be profaned, speakers substituted *Adonai*, which means Lord. This ancient practice is reflected in the familiar pronunciation we gave the Tetragrammaton in the New Jerusalem Bible. Combining the vowels of *Adonai* with the four Hebrew consonants, YHWH, God's name was pronounced "Jehovah." Today, we more often speak it as *Yahweh*. Because this name of God was sacred to the Hebrew readers, they continue to substitute "Lord" for YHWH in the text. If we look in the Old Testament and turn to Psalm 23, we will see in the first sentence that "LORD" is printed with small caps. This practice of using small-capped letters is how the writers expressed YHWH, the sacred name of God.

In the New Testament, when Jesus is called Lord, he is being called God. "Jesus is Lord" is a faith statement and a theological truth for Christians. YHWH means "I am" in its simplest form. Jesus boldly announces who he is through the "I am" sayings in the Gospel of John. **I am the Bread of Life. I am the Way. I am the Good Shepherd. I am the Resurrection and the Life.** "I am" was an intentional and poorly disguised message announcing Jesus' real identity to his hearers. When we say Jesus is Lord, it means we look to him as our God. His life, death, and resurrection give proof of his saving love and his claim to be our Lord and our God.

Each of us will have to choose what we believe sometime in our lives. We will have to choose which religious beliefs we will follow. Many of us revisit our faith statements from time to time. Some may choose not to believe in God at all. Others will choose a spiritual path based on what makes them feel good at the moment. But at some point we each will have to choose what we believe.

Some astounding news emerged in the aftermath of the tragic auto accident that killed Princess Diana. The chauffeur of the car had three times the legal blood-alcohol level. The police estimate that her limousine was traveling at about one hundred and twenty miles per hour when the crash occurred in a Paris tunnel. Clearly the wrong man was driving the princess.

Celebrities might spend $150,000 to $200,000 on a custom-built limo but it is not that uncommon for them to hire a driver without adequate training. No doubt after Diana's death more celebrities started to pay more attention to the quality of the person they entrust with their lives.

The same wisdom has to be used when we choose the religious beliefs that steer our lives. The issue is not whether our religion makes us feel warm and fuzzy. The only concern should be with whether it is true, trustworthy, meaningful in our lives now, and able to bring us to our hoped-for destination in the life to come. When we claim that Jesus is our Savior & Lord, we are once again claiming what we believe and in whom we trust with our life and soul. For me, saying Jesus is my Savior & Lord reaches straight into my chest and grabs my heart with what I need to know is true and sense as real. It is what gives me hope and courage to be his disciple. Yes, Jesus is Savior & Lord.

27
Come, Go, Come Again
Acts 1:6–11

Q. 29. What does it mean that Jesus ascended into heaven?

A. 29. After his work on earth was done, he returned to heaven to prepare a place for us and to rule with God in love. He will come again in glory, and remains with us now through the gift of the Holy Spirit.

According to Luke, the resurrected Jesus was enveloped by a cloud and lifted up to heaven from atop the Mount of Olives near the village of Bethany. It happened forty days after Easter and ten days before the Jewish holiday of Pentecost. The event was witnessed by the remaining eleven apostles and most likely a number of his followers. It is one of a handful of mystical events in the life of Jesus. As in Jesus' transfiguration, when Jesus went up on a mountaintop to counsel with Moses and Elijah, or his encounter with the devil in the Jordanian hills, mystery surrounded this event. Like his walking on water, the story of Jesus' ascension to heaven is not an easy one to explain rationally. Because this is a mystical event, many myths have arisen around the story, including speculation on the exact location of the mystical happening.

It was our second full day in Jerusalem and our itinerary called for us forty pilgrims to wake up early and to be ready for the bus by 7 A.M. for our tour around the Holy Land. The Seven Arches Hotel was located at the south end of the Mount of Olives, overlooking the many graveyards in the Kidron Valley. This meant that it was just a short ride to our first stop, the shrine, just outside of Bethany, now in a Palestinian neighborhood, where tradition has it that our Lord Jesus ascended to heaven. The small circular stone chapel stood within a fenced-in courtyard. The gate was locked. We patiently stood at the entrance as the bus driver, a Palestinian Muslim, knocked on doors of the homes in the Palestinian neighborhood adjacent to the shrine, looking for the caretaker. As he knocked on doors, a vagrant approached our group. His dress marked him as a street person and his face revealed the desperation of his life. He was begging for coins from Americans. In his hand was a plastic bag containing six used syringes, which he waved in the faces of his captive audience. He poked a prescription at our tour guide, who spoke to him in

Arabic. It quickly became a shoving and shouting match, with the man uttering profanities. We found refuge in the courtyard of the Shrine of the Ascension before the man went on his way.

The chapel was so small that only one or two persons could enter at a time. Our guide was inside describing the scene for each pilgrim. Under a domed ceiling was the crest of the Mount of Olives, an outcrop of bare rock. The rock was shiny from pilgrims rubbing it over the centuries. John, our guide, explained that we know that this is the spot where Jesus left the earth because we can see the impression his foot left in the rock. He told us that this footprint is his last bodily mark on earth, until he comes again in glory.

Sure enough, if you let your imagination loose, you can convince yourself that the impression in the rock is a footprint, about a size nine. There is no logical explanation of how his foot left an imprint in solid rock, just the centuries-old claim that this is the place. And just like the rest of the pilgrims from our bus (and hundreds of thousands before us), I had to put my foot in the mark to say that I stood where Jesus last stood on earth at the moment that the cloud enveloped him and he ascended into heaven.

Scripture tells us that Jesus would come, go, and come again. Christmas marks the first coming, the Ascension marks his going, and sometime in the future he will come again in glory. Some Bible scholars, including William Barclay, explain that the event of the Ascension shows that the resurrected Jesus actually left the earth. It marks an ending. We could not just say that he faded away or grew tired of appearing. His earthly mission had to have a final moment in history. This end began yet another chapter, in which the Holy Spirit brought in the age of the church.

Other scholars emphasize the mystical nature of the event. Just as Jesus arrived on earth accompanied by angels declaring his identity (Luke 2:11), he left the earth with angels announcing that this same One would return: "Why are you just standing here, looking up? Don't you have work to do? He'll be back!" (Acts 1:11, paraphr.).

They say the cloud was not a cumulus or nimbus or stratus, but the *Shekinah* of Glory, the actual presence of God, kept hidden from human eyes so that the onlooker would not be struck dead. In Old Testament times, the *Shekinah* was described as a cloud or glowing aura like that surrounding the bush that flamed but did not burn up. The Ascension marks the reality of Jesus' entrance into the heavenly presence of the Almighty; it was a transition from his earthly role to a higher heavenly status of being seated at the Father's right hand, which traditionally symbolizes the locus of divine power. Scholars say that the symbolism of God's right hand, the power side of God, demonstrates that Jesus is still in control of the world that he has physically left behind. His power is felt through his Spirit, who has taken the place of his bodily presence. He is still with us, through his Spiritual presence. We celebrate and acknowledge this in the sacrament of the Lord's Supper.

An ancient Ascension Day hymn, *Deus ascendit*, or "God Has Gone Up," reminds the church that he has ascended, *not gone away*, in order to be the empowerment of the church until this era ends.[34] A few scholars, however, question the historicity of the event. They call it an invention of Luke to explain the theological and spiritual truths that Christ was exalted and now is in God's realm rather than the human experience.[35] That conclusion is too crude and unfair to Luke for me to accept. When Luke wrote his Gospel, there were still many eyewitnesses to this event. If Luke had made it up, they would have challenged him. At the same time, we are cautioned not to take the story too literally and draw from it a sense that Jesus went away to a place in space. We are dealing with a mystical, supernatural event, the explanation of which has to use anthropomorphic terms and concepts. Only God can fully describe what happened.

For the contemporary church, the Ascension of Jesus marks the in-between time, the era between his going and his coming in glory. Theology calls this the Church Age. It is not just a time to wait around; it is a time for activity! The angels challenged the apostles, "Why are you just standing there, looking up? You have work to do before he comes back." Ten days later, the power of Christ's Spirit thundered into the hearts of the believers and to this day has made what we do in Jesus' name very special.

In a statement approved in June 2002 by the PC(USA) General Assembly, called "Hope in the Lord Jesus Christ," Presbyterians are reminded that "The power of the Holy Spirit leads the whole community of faith into holy and joyful living, enabling each of us to conform our lives more fully to Christ. Christians are called to live by the Spirit, forsaking works of the flesh and receiving the fruit of the Spirit."[36]

During the in-between time, when Christ is in the heavenly realm, the Holy Spirit is with the church and with each believer, active behind the scenes of history, leading the human experience in the direction of God's will. As believers, we are to work for the reconciliation of the world, empowered by Christ's Spirit, which is made know to us in dozens of ways, including the power and peace we often sense as God working in our lives.

Country singer Susan Ashton tells how God arranged for her to sing about her faith in a setting she never imagined possible. The story is that Garth Brooks's brother Kelly dated a woman who liked Ashton's music. One day, after Kelly's girlfriend played an Ashton CD for him, he called his famous brother and told him he should take Susan Ashton on tour with him. So he did! Ashton was fearful that people who wanted to hear Garth Brooks might boo her off the stage. She sang her songs and shared her faith in God and received a standing ovation. When she got to know Garth Brooks better, he admitted to her that he had not heard her sing until she stepped on stage that first night on tour. That night, he had been floored. He fell in love with her voice and found her lyrics moving.

You may not have the opportunity to sing gospel songs in front of fifty thousand people, but God will put you in situations you could not imagine, in which people will be open to hearing about your faith in God. The possibilities are wide-ranging: the stranger next to you on a flight, fellow parents at a PTA meeting, a new employee in the next cubicle, the kids you coach or teach or drive to school. In this in-between time, the Holy Spirit of Jesus is the power putting you where God wants you to be.

One of the most striking images of the war in Vietnam is that of a black-haired girl wearing no clothes and brutally burned from a napalm attack on her village, running down a road. The raid had killed two of her brothers. I understand that the little girl in the picture is now a Christian and hopes that the historic photograph can be used to foster peace in the world. The ones who suffer the most are often the world's greatest peacemakers. Peacemaking is a calling instituted by Jesus when he spoke a sermon on a hill along the Sea of Galilee.

In this in-between time, the Holy Spirit of Jesus empowers little girls, scarred by war, to work for peace in a world that seems hungry for more violence. The same Holy Spirit calls you and me to do what we can to work for peace among neighbors, strangers, family, races, and nations to ready this world for the return of the Son of God, who will come in glory.

The church in these in-between times is challenged to work for peace and reconciliation of the world to God. And we have the tools to do it: power, prayer, and peace of our Lord Jesus Christ.

28

Blow, Spirit, Blow

Acts 2:1-4

"Blow, Spirit, blow over the face of earth." And life stirred in the breeze of God. (Gen. 1—2, paraphr.)

"Blow, Spirit, blow over the heads of believers." And life stirred in the breeze of God. (Acts 2:2, paraphr.)

"Blow, Spirit, blow over the minds of doubters. You may not know from where it blows but know that it is the breeze of God." (John 3:8, paraphr.)

"When the Feast of Pentecost came, they were all together in one place. Without warning there was a sound like a strong wind, gale force—no one could tell where it came from. It filled the whole building. Then, like a wildfire, the Holy Spirit spread through their ranks, and they started speaking in a number of different languages as the Spirit prompted them." (Acts 2:1–4, *The Message*)

In Hebrew the word for spirit means breeze, wind, or breath. In New Testament Greek, the word for spirit means the same things, and when it is spoken in a religious sense spirit often means "the presence of God."

**Q. 30. When was the Holy Spirit given to the
first Christians?**

A. 30. On the day of Pentecost.

Q. 31. What happened on the day of Pentecost?

**A. 31. When the first Christians met together in
Jerusalem, the Holy Spirit came upon them like a
mighty wind. They all began to speak in different
languages. A crowd gathered in astonishment. Peter
preached to them the gospel.**

The contemporary catechism condenses the second chapter of Acts down to four short statements. But if we look at the story as we find it in the text, surprisingly there are nine key points in just the first four verses, the most important of which is found at the end of verse four.

Just for fun, if I were teaching this passage in a Bible study setting, it would go something like this:

"When the day of Pentecost had come . . ." We are talking about patience. Jesus had told his disciples to wait in Jerusalem for the Spirit to come to them. It is so hard to wait. I hate it when I have to wait. Often I will just go on and do something instead, when I should have waited for a better time. I hate that I do not like to wait. I am sure that the apostles who, after the mystical experience of seeing Jesus whisked to heaven on a cloud, wanted to move out into their region immediately. Instead they did as Jesus wished them to do, and waited. They waited an hour, then a day, a week. They waited ten days.

We are told, in one of the most profound and poetic passages of Isaiah, that "those who wait for the LORD shall renew their strength, they shall mount up with wings like eagles" (Isa. 40:31). Wait for God and for God's timing and you, too, shall mount up with wings like eagles.

"They were all together in one place." This indicates that the believers had a unity of purpose that transcended their personal differences and kept them in fellowship. Jesus was gone; who knew what to expect next? Tempting as it may have been for them to go their own ways, they stayed together. My friends, stay in community!

"And suddenly . . . from heaven there came a sound like the rush of a violent wind." Life with God is always filled with surprises. *Suddenly,* out of the blue, from nowhere, unexpectedly it came. And because they were together in one place, they all got to see it happen in one another's lives. What a thrill! For you to see God at work in a friend's life and for that friend to see God at work in your life is an awesome two-for-one spiritual bargain!

"And it filled the entire house where they were." The power of God's presence is all-encompassing—a *total* experience! The Spirit *filled* the house! God fills each believer with grace until our cup overflows! Jesus explained it like this: "A good measure, pressed down, shaken together, running over, will be put into your lap; for the measure you give will be the measure you get back (Luke 6:38)."

"Tongues, as of fire." The Holy Spirit is at work in us so that others can see it. Not so that we can take pride in it, but so that God's will is done through us. Maybe it will be a strong voice when others are silent. Or a compassionate touch when others refrain from getting too close to someone regarded as untouchable. Maybe it will be an impromptu sharing of faith. Maybe swallowing hard and saying, "I'm sorry," and seeing the cold, hard barrier between us and a loved one crumble like Jericho's walls. Or how about when people remark on our strength when we know that we are about to faint? Remember, "they shall run and not be weary, they shall walk and not faint" (Isa. 40:31). The Holy Spirit is at work in our lives, and others will notice!

"A tongue of fire rested on each of them." On whom? Only on the apostles, on the rich, on the men? No, on each one of them! The gift of the Holy Spirit is given to every Christian believer. We acknowledge the wondrous imposition of the Holy Spirit at our baptism. We do not have to have a special experience or a deeper understanding or even a holier life to have the Holy Spirit enter us. Rather, the Spirit of God is present in each believer, even before we realize it. God's Spirit is in us.

"All of them were filled with the Holy Spirit." Again, we find the word *filled*. It must be an important word. The Holy Spirit of God works in a holistic fashion in each of us. It's not just a mind thing or just a soul thing. It is an every-thing! Heart, mind, soul, strength, dreams, loves, job, children, home, work, play, art, attitude, political views, one's checkbook and 401Ks. God is in it all working God's ways in our lives. God is involved with all of us. It is not just a spirit thing; it is an every-thing!

"Began to speak in other languages . . . . " When God's Spirit is working in us, God will find ways to make our witness useful so that others who can be especially helped by our particular faith story or by our Christian presence can hear and feel it as needed.

Jewish pilgrims from all over the Roman Empire were in Jerusalem on Pentecost to worship God. Each one who heard Peter's famous Pentecost sermon heard the gospel message in a language he could understand.[37] God found a way to communicate the good news so that it would affect each man's heart at the place of greatest need. God will find ways to make our witness effective.

And now comes the critical message to the contemporary church: They spoke **"as the Spirit gave them the ability."** God gives us the ability to live and share in ways that exemplify the gospel, if we are receptive to the Holy Spirit leading us. When we are amenable to God's Spirit working in our lives, amazing things happen and lives are blessed.

I received an e-mail from an active member who has been with the church I serve since the church's struggling early days in the 1960s. She has served as an elder, clerk of the session, and a church school teacher and was on the search committee that brought me to the church. So as you can imagine, when she suggests something, I willingly and eagerly listen.

What she found was a brief article in a recent denominational mass e-mailing that suggested local churches should experiment with a renewal of baptism service in small group gatherings and meetings. She liked that idea and wondered if Presbyterians did such things and if I might consider something like this for the church. I wrote back telling her that, yes, it *was* something Presbyterians do and have been doing for some time. In fact, we have a series of suggested formats for such services in our *Book of Common Worship*. I thanked her for the heads-up on the article and told her that I was planning a sermon on baptism in a few weeks and that she gave me an idea of what we could do.

Her e-mail really did spark ideas, and my brain roared into action. I was preaching a series on the sacraments and in two weeks I would be dealing with baptism. I had never led a renewal of baptism service at this church and really felt the Holy Spirit nudge me in that direction. The ideas flowed like a spring flash flood. I created an order of worship using the prayers and words found in the *Book of Common Worship* and after a sermon about the meaning and practice of baptism, I wrote out a renewal of baptism with an option for worshipers to come forward and have a cross traced on the forehead with the water from the baptism font. Writing out the service came fast and furious and I handed it to Tricia, the church secretary, for typing.

But as the week closed in on Sunday, I began to wonder if this was too radical for our church. Doubts like this usually come when it's too late to change anything, and that makes them even more disturbing. Then I wondered if anyone would even come forward, which would make me and Dick, our minister of visitation who was to assist that day, look like sore thumbs sticking out of a poorly devised plan. But it was too late to change anything in the bulletin, so the ushers filled the baptism font and the service began.

To make a long and worrisome story short, the hymn was sung, the printed prayers and affirmations were said, and the invitation made for Presbyterians to come forward and have their foreheads wetted with a cool trace of the cross. Dick and I stood ready, but also ready in case no one rose from the chairs to come forward. Out of the corner of my eye, I saw Steve walking up the aisle, a lone man among hundreds of bowed heads. Then Marc, then Georgia. As they come forward, Dick and I said the blessing suggested by the *Book of Common Worship*, *"Remember your baptism and be thankful. In the name of the Father and of the Son and of the Holy Spirit"*

The lines lengthened and the hymn's verses were exhausted. The organist continued to play softy. Choir members in their robes approached. Visitors in worship bowed their unfamiliar faces as I blessed them. Some made eye contact while others closed their eyes for the blessing and touch. Some had tears in their eyes as they came forward, while others, I'm told, had tears come to their eyes on the way back to their seats. Little children, teenagers and older adults looked up at me in eager anticipation. I knew most of their names so I used the name they were given in baptism as I blessed them. For over ten minutes, about 150 worshipers renewed their baptism and touched their pastors' hearts with the worshipers' humility and faith. After the service, Dick said to me that in his years as a pastor and an army chaplain, he had never experienced a renewal service like this one. It was awesome, I agreed.

When we let the Spirit lead and trust that leading to take us on a godly adventure, we will not be disappointed. It is truly amazing what takes place when we open ourselves to the Holy Spirit and let faith take our hand.

God gives us the ability to live in ways that exemplify the gospel, if we are receptive to the Holy Spirit leading us. When we are amenable to the Spirit of God working in our lives,

amazing things can happen,
lives are blessed,
others see God at work in us,
God's grace overflows,

we will find effective ways to share the love of God,
we will enjoy being in community,
and Christian living will be a total experience.

Blow, Spirit, blow over your people today and let them receive the breeze of God!

29
What Is the Gospel?
John 3:15; Acts 2:28; Romans 6:23

L ast week we explored the power-producing moment the Holy Spirit came to the first Christians. In Acts 2, one of the first results of the coming of the Spirit was that Peter preached the gospel to a large crowd, and about three thousand people became believers. This leads to the next question in the contemporary catechism. What precisely *is* the gospel that he preached?

Q. 32. What is the gospel?

A. 32. The gospel is the good news about Jesus. It promises us the forgiveness of our sins and eternal life because of him. Forgiveness and eternal life with God are what we mean by salvation.

The meaning of the word "gospel" may be confusing. In church-talk we use the word in two different ways. *Gospel* (with a capital G) is used to refer to the first four books of the New Testament. The official terminology is: The Gospel according to Matthew; The Gospel according to Mark; The Gospel according to Luke; The Gospel according to John. These are not the original titles of the Gospels. In fact, like other manuscripts from that time and place, the Greek manuscripts did not have titles or bylines at all. We are not quite sure exactly who wrote the four accounts of Jesus' life. Early theologians gave Matthew, Mark, Luke, and John author's credit for different reasons, some historically valid and others less so.

Matthew, Mark, and Luke are called the Synoptic Gospels, meaning that they are "viewed together" because they have a similar narrative style. Today, biblical scholars believe that there were four original written sources from which the Synoptic Gospel writers got their material.

- A Mark source: Material believed to have been gleaned from Peter's stories.
- A Luke source: Material that is found only in Luke's Gospel.
- A Matthew source: Material that is original with Matthew's Gospel.
- A collection of Jesus' sayings: The Q source. The name Q is shorthand for *Quelle,* the German word for source. Q is a collection of sayings that date from about eighteen years after Jesus' death.

Mark wrote his account of Jesus' life from his own collection of material that may have been Peter's reports. Matthew used Mark, the Q source, and his own material to form his Gospel. Luke used Mark, the Q source, and the material he collected himself to write his Gospel. This multilayered collection of stories and data is the most likely explanation for the many similarities and differences among the three Synoptic Gospels. John's Gospel was written much later, and it is quite different in content and theology from the Synoptic Gospels. Matthew, Mark, and Luke tell the story of Jesus pointing to God, and John the story of God pointing to Jesus.

When we use the word Gospel with a capital G we are talking about the written accounts of Jesus' life, death, and resurrection. But gospel means more than just the four written accounts of Jesus' life. The gospel, with a small "g," means good news or glad tidings. Its root is used as a verb to mean to preach or to tell good news about God. The word "gospel" comes from an Anglo-Saxon word, godspell, that means "good story" or "good news." The Broadway play takes its name from this ancient word, interpreting it as a story about God.

The story we tell is a supernatural account of God becoming a human being in Jesus of Nazareth. By his life, death, and resurrection, Jesus Christ gave the world the opportunity to be forgiven and to find eternal life. The gospel is the saving message of Jesus with the power to change hearts and transform lives. The gospel is not a human discovery of what God is doing. Rather, it is God letting us know what God is doing in the world.

For those of us who like to hear how theologians say it, the *Interpreter's Dictionary of the Bible* explains gospel in relation to slavery. Human beings are slaves to cosmic forces. But the gospel announces that now through God's redemptive work, we have been delivered from the bondage, which made it impossible for us to lead a true life. "This is the historical fact, which is essential for the working out of God's redemptive purpose."[38]

I like to think about it in a much simpler way. The gospel is God's gift of grace in Jesus Christ. When we open the gift, we find **forgiveness** and **eternal life**. These are two gifts we all crave yet often wonder if they are real for us. Am I **forgiven?**

We trust God to forgive us yet often continue to be haunted by memories of hurtful things we have done. For those times, it may be helpful to think about forgiveness as if it were a church bell. The church I served in western Pennsylvania had one of the few working church bells in the area. We arranged for a teenager to ring the bell each week as church let out. It was a heavy bell and the rope was thick. It took a hard series of pulls to get it going. One time my son Kiel had the honor. He was new to the job, and when he pulled on the rope the bell leaned down and then up again with such a force that he was pulled high into the hallway—he had forgotten to let go! When he did, he was fifteen feet in the air. He hit hard. We ended up in the emergency room to have his knee x-rayed. Once the bell started to ring, the teens were to let go of the rope. Yet the bell continued to rock and ring until it slowed down.

If we have been tugging at our sinful actions and attitudes, we should not be surprised if the consequences and shameful feelings continue to rise to the surface, even after we have let go and asked God to forgive us. These are the natural reverberations of behavior and attitudes that have been left at the feet of Christ. We are forgiven, yet it may take some time for the echoes to fade away from our active conscience. Although we crave forgiveness and eternal life, we often wonder if they are real for us.

Allen is a good friend of mine and is now serving a church in Davidson, North Carolina. He tells a story about a grieving widower on the day of his wife's funeral. The husband and Allen were walking back from the graveside to the parked cars. The grieving husband pulled Allen aside and said, "Allen, thank you for those wonderful words. But now it is just you and I. Tell me, is my wife in heaven, or is she back there in that grave? What do you really believe?"

Allen remarked: "Now that's being put on the spot." After taking a moment to collect his thoughts he said, "My friend, there are many things I wonder about. There are some parts of the Bible I cannot accept at face value. There are some doctrines I doubt and there are some questions I'll never have answered. But this I do believe: Jesus died and rose again, and it will be the same for those who have died in Jesus. Your wife believed in him, and did the best she could to follow him. God keeps his promises, and your wife is not back there in the grave; she has already known the joy of the resurrection."

The gospel assures us of eternal life and forgiveness. Thanks be to God!

30

It Must Be the Spirit!

Acts 4:31–35; Romans 8:11; Ephesians 4:4–6

This meditation links two questions from the contemporary catechism because they deal with the same topic in a "then and now" sort of way.

Then:

Q. 33. What were the results of Pentecost?

A. 33. The Holy Spirit filled the first Christians with joy by revealing what Jesus had done for us. The Spirit inspired them to understand and proclaim the gospel, and to live a new life together in thanksgiving to God.

Now:

Q. 34. How do these results continue today?

A. 34. The Holy Spirit also moves us to understand and believe the gospel, gives us strength and wisdom to live by it, and unites us into a new community called the church.

Blending these two faith statements together, we get a concise picture of what the Holy Spirit does for believers. The Holy Spirit fills us with joy, inspires us to understand the gospel, and to share it and live it out, and it unites all believers as the community called the church.

The Holy Spirit fills us with joy. A friend once told me that there is a difference between happiness and joy. She said happiness is a goal that people strive to reach. We hear people say, "I'm doing this because it will make me happy." Another expression is "I'll be happy if . . . ." Although people strive toward happiness as a goal, this goal is one that tends never to be reached. Those who try hard to make themselves happy often are the saddest people on earth. Happiness seems always just out of reach.

Joy, on the other hand, is a state of being. It is an inner awareness of peace and trust in God. Joy is a matter of the heart, while happiness is more often a future state of mind. Those who know the joy of the Lord can experience the deepest sorrows, the cruelest insults, the most painful let downs, but still have joy in their heart. I have seen it often among church members. With cheeks still wet with tears, a member will say something like, "Yet isn't God good!" or "But I'm so fortunate to have so many people who love me!" or "The Lord will see me through this." Often a smile emerges as the words are coming out. This behavior is evidence of being filled with joy. The Holy Spirit fills us with joy.

The Holy Spirit inspires us to understand, tell, and live out the gospel. To understand, tell about, and live out the gospel requires help. The Holy Spirit helps us to understand because often we simply do not. A teacher caught a little boy saying a swear word.

"Where did you learn a word like that?"

"My daddy said it."

"Even so, you don't even know what it means," said the teacher.

"I do too," the boy said. "It means the car won't start."

How often do we assume that we know what the Spirit of Christ is trying to do in our lives, but get mixed up or just simply do not know how the gospel empowers our lives? The Holy Spirit inspires us to understand the gospel.

And the Holy Spirit inspires us to tell the gospel. We all need the Spirit's help in our evangelism efforts. I heard about a new minister who worked all week on his first sermon. He edited it, typed it out and highlighted it, left it on his desk all ready for Sunday. On Saturday, the sexton cleaned the church and accidentally threw away the sermon. When the minister saw that the sermon was gone, he panicked. He looked everywhere for it, but it was gone. Too late to write up another, he told the congregation, "I had a nice sermon prepared for you this morning, but when I got to church it was gone. I'm going to have to rely on the inspiration of the Spirit today, but I promise to do better next Sunday."

I have been preaching for twenty-five years, and I know it must be the inspiration of the Holy Spirit that makes my sermons meaningful. Often, worshipers will come up to me after worship and tell me how the sermon impacted their lives. Sometimes worshipers will say that I must have been reading their minds. My usual response is to say thanks, and that it must be the Holy Spirit at work. I really believe the Holy Spirit does something to my words between my mouth and worshipers' ears. The Holy Spirit makes the sermon the word of God. This is the only explanation that makes sense to me.

The Holy Spirit inspires us to understand, tell, and live out the gospel. Paul says that if the Spirit of Christ lives in you, you will be able to live out the gospel (Rom. 8:11, paraphr.).

And the Holy Spirit unites us in a community called the Church. The apostle Paul put it this way: "There's just one body and just one Spirit, one hope, one Lord, one faith, one baptism, one God who is in all things" (Eph. 4:4–6, paraphr.). The word "exclusive" would not be in Paul's vocabulary. Occasionally churches are guilty of displaying this detestable word on their front signs.

The big names of the Protestant Reformation are well-known: They include forerunners such as Hus and Savonarola, then Luther, Calvin, Knox, and Zwingli. There is another voice, however, that had much to say, although few today know his name. He was the chief associate of the German Reformer Martin Luther. His name is Philip Melanchthon. In a day of major and far-reaching theological battles and assaults from the Roman Church as well as between the schools of Reformers themselves, "the gentleman reformer," as he was known, summed up the attitude we need to have in the church. His theology can be expressed in the motto "In essentials, unity; in nonessentials, liberty; in all things, charity." There is no better motto than this when it comes to the unity of the church.

The Lord's Prayer is a constant reminder to be united in Christ. Every time we pray the Lord's Prayer, the Holy Spirit teaches us about unity. There is no "I" in the prayer nor is there a "my." When we pray it, we automatically pray for others and their needs. When we pray it, I hope we notice that it never says "me."

Jack Haberer, a friend of mine and a pastor in Houston, wrote in the *Presbyterian Outlook Online* about the real plus of being part of the Presbyterian community of faith. He acknowledged that it is not always easy to rub shoulders with those who may have vastly differing viewpoints on doctrine or worship style, but he says that really does not matter.

> The power of Presbyterian connectionalism is the convenantal relationship we all entered into in our baptism. A spirit of intentional, authentic accountability animates such a connection between us. Indeed, part of its wonder is the reality that by becoming a Presbyterian one enters into mutual accountability with people, many of which we never would have chosen as friends. But the choosing is on God's side. Fact is, we have been made sisters and brothers by God's doing, so we are obligated to act as family—the healthy kind of family that speaks the truth in love, while living in close proximity to one another."[39]

The Holy Spirit unites us as a faith community called *the church*. It is an inclusive community. But there is always a temptation to think that some of those who are here do not really belong. The Holy Spirit reminds us that not only do we sometimes think that way about others but that they may be thinking that about us. So thank God for grace and the Spirit of Christ, who unites us as the church, a family of faith that can speak the truth in love and allow us to love in spite of our differences.

31

What Is the Church?

1 Corinthians 12:4-7, 12-13; Ephesians 3:14-19

A s Presbyterians we have come to believe that if you are a Christian, you will be active in a church. It is like peanut butter and jelly; the two just go together naturally. If you are a Christian, your life will not be complete unless you worship with the people of God. If you are a churchgoer, Christ must be at work in you. We believe you cannot be a solitary Christian, a Lone Ranger. Belonging to the community of faith is a natural by-product and benefit of being a Christian.

You may recall the riddle: What is missing from CH__CH? The two-letter answer is: UR. When you are missing from church, as a believer you are really missing out on a key blessing and opportunity of the Faith! When someone has fallen out of the habit of regular worship or turned his or her back on the church, it is a spiritual crisis. Often something dramatic is needed to bring that person back to the company of Christians.

Q. 35. What is the church?

A. 35. We are the church: the people who believe the good news about Jesus, who are baptized, and who share in the Lord's Supper. Through these means of grace, the Spirit renews us so that we may serve God in love.

The contemporary catechism highlights five actions that mark the church as a special gathering of people. Church people believe the good news of Jesus, are baptized, share the Lord's Supper, are renewed by God's grace, serve God in love. The church is a lot more than these five actions, of course, but church would not be the church if any one of these were missing.

First, if our belief in the good news were missing, we would be like Edmund, one of the four children who visited the magical land of Narnia, in C. S. Lewis's book *The Lion, the Witch and the Wardrobe*. The wicked White Queen enticed Edmund with Turkish delights. Each piece of candy was sweet and delicious, and Edmund had never tasted anything better. He kept eating them because they were so tasty. Unfortunately, he did not know that the more of them he ate, the more he would want, and that he would eat until it killed him. The candy would never satisfy his hunger; it would never fill him up; it would simply destroy him.

Without the satisfying good news of Jesus, we would keep looking for more things to fill up our lives, more experiences and people to fill the holes, to satisfy us, to give us fulfillment and to help us find meaning. They never seem to do the trick. The goodies in life were never meant to fill us up or give us lasting satisfaction. The things of this world are not eternal. Only God can satisfy the deepest desires of our heart, and that's the good news of Jesus Christ! The church believes the good news of the gospel!

Second, without baptism, we would never be able to identify the point at which we began our journey of faith. Jesus started his journey in the waters of the Jordan. I started my journey in the waters of the Church of the Nativity in Midland Park, New Jersey, in 1954. Charlie, a month-old baby, started his journey of faith two weeks ago when I baptized him at church. Without baptism, we could never say where or when our faith journey began.

In baptism, we become family. In baptism we are called to ministry. In baptism we are given a name that marks us for life as a child of God. In baptism we receive the Holy Spirit. In baptism we tell the world that we are Christ's. In baptism we acknowledge that we are sinners in need of forgiveness. In baptism we become the company of saints. Baptism marks the start of our Christian journey, and the gathering of baptized saints.

Third, without the sharing of the Lord's Supper, it would be easy for us as a church to think that all the resources for holy living are warehoused in the human heart and that nothing more is needed. Each time we approach the Lord's Table, we are revealing to ourselves, and to those who share the meal with us, that we are needy, spiritually needy. We hunger for more of God. Communion is intentionally a public event! It shows others that everyone needs God. No one is exempt from the need of grace; no one is too high in rank or too lost in sin to be left out of, or beyond the possibility of, renewal.

While serving as a chaplain in a unit of the United States Army Medical Group, I conducted a Communion service that I remember well, because it seemed to create worshipers in shock. A full colonel headed our unit, and he had been selected for promotion to general. He was a well-known physician, an orthopedic surgeon who was one of the team doctors for the Pittsburgh Pirates baseball team during spring training in Florida. He was also a Presbyterian elder. I set up my chaplain's kit on the hood of a jeep. The chalice, bread tray, candles, and the white napkins that covered the elements fit neatly on the hood, just as they were designed to do. I brought out folding chairs from the HQ tent and made rows for our service. The unit gathered and we sang some easy songs. They listened to Scripture and I preached and we prayed. Only the colonel was Presbyterian and many did not attend church regularly, so I explained that Communion is a time when we come to God in spiritual need and leave filled with God's grace. I emphasized the need for a humble spirit in approaching God, in both those serving and those partaking of the elements. I explained that those serving are not of a higher status or rank, but in fact are in the role of humble and lowly servants.

I called the elder forward to assist me in serving the bread and cup. With head lowered in prayer, Colonel Springer got up from his folding chair, took the bread plate from the hood of the jeep, and turned toward the men and women of the unit. I can still see their expressions of shock, amazement, and puzzlement. I can still hear their unspoken thoughts:

"He is going to serve me?"

"I'm just a private. Isn't he almost a general?"

"I'm a sergeant and I can't have this future general serving me!"

One by one, they came forward, took the bread while Colonel Springer said, "The body of Christ," then dipped it in the cup of altar wine I was holding, received Communion, and returned to their chairs. In that moment, there were no stripes or bars or oak clusters or future stars; there were only brothers and sisters in Christ, equally hungering for the egalitarian grace that comes every time we gather at the Lord's Table. The church shares the Lord's Supper as fellow saints in need of renewal.

Fourth, the church is constantly renewed by God's grace. The apostle Paul explained it using these words:

> My response is to get down on my knees before the Father. . . . I ask him to strengthen you by his Spirit—not a brute strength but a glorious inner strength—that Christ will live in you as you open the door and invite him in. And I ask him that with both feet planted firmly on love, you'll be able to take in with all Christians the extravagant dimensions of Christ's love. Reach out and experience the breadth! Test its length! Plumb the depths! Rise to the heights! Live full lives, full in the fullness of God.
>
> God can do anything, you know—far more than you could ever imagine or guess or request in your wildest dreams! [He] does it not by pushing us around but by working within us, his Spirit deeply and gently within us. Glory to God in the church![40]

Fifth, the church serves God in love. It is the time of year at my church when we recruit new deacons and elders to serve as church leaders for the next three years. The first thing I will say to a candidate is that, yes, you are a leader, but you will be a servant leader. The privilege will be to serve, not to be served. The basin and towel symbolize the power of church leadership. Jesus humbly bent down and washed the feet of his disciples. The late Dr. Bruce Thielemann, former dean of the chapel at Grove City College in Pennsylvania, coined the term "basin theology." Basin theology derives from Jesus' model of leadership. Church leaders serve the members. Church leaders follow basin theology.

Maybe one of the most striking examples of basin theology comes from a well-known story told about a Japanese Christian leader and author who was on a speaking tour of America. At a national convention of pastors, he and the denominational officials who escorted him stopped in the restroom. As often happens at large conventions, many who had used the restroom that day had missed the trash can with their paper towels. When the speaker's escorts left the restroom, they could not find the honored guest. Looking around, they went back into the restroom and saw this famous Christian leader carefully picking up all the paper towels that others had left for the maintenance crew to clean up.

Is anything beneath our dignity if the church genuinely desires to serve God in love? The whole church needs to practice basin theology, because the church is called to serve God in love. What is the church? Is it a collection of perfect saints? Not by a long shot. It is a collection of people who believe the good news, observe the sacraments, are renewed weekly, and serve God in love.

32

What Is My Only Comfort?

Romans 8:38-39

What can we count on, for sure? Things break or wear out. Roofs leak. Faucets drip. Bells tarnish. Pianos go out of tune. The Dow goes down. Dot.coms come and go. We cannot count on material things to last.

A man collected his pennies for over forty years—two hundred and sixty thousand of them. Last week he cashed them in. All that effort and time only netted him $2,600. It seems as though he should have gotten more for his forty years of effort. Can we count on money to satisfy or last? We can try.

We cannot count on television news. The aunt of one of the snipers in the Washington, D.C., area in the last decade told about her experience raising the young boy. During the exclusive interview, the woman exclaimed that the man was really good and that she still loved him and hoped God would turn his life around. The interview with the brokenhearted woman went on for ten minutes. When it was over, the woman interrupted the host to confess that she really was not the aunt who raised him, but that she had married into the family only recently, and that she had known the convicted man for only a brief time. We expect legitimate news, but we cannot count on it.

Friends let us down. We can't always depend on family. The church can disappoint us. One time the church let me down and it hurt. It was stewardship time. Things were going well and we had plans for some innovative programs at church. I had been serving this congregation for just over a year, and I was enjoying my ministry there. The leadership was excited, and we challenged the congregation with a good-sized budget increase that included a small cost-of-living raise for the staff. A trustee was to give a stewardship talk in worship, encouraging the church to stretch and give and to help the church do some new things. He was a well-respected businessman, a long-time church member and, I thought, gracious, savvy, and wise. I could not think of a better choice to give an upbeat stewardship talk. As I sat in the chancel chair he took the pulpit and pulled out his notes. He told the church that our proposed budget was bigger than ever and that people needed to give more to the church. Then he said, "Everybody knows that our last pastor never asked for a raise in the nine years he served our church. Our new minister has asked for a raise and that's a big part of the increase in our budget." When he sat down, he leaned over and in a semi-apologetic way whispered to me, "I guess I should have warned you about what I was going to say." Sometimes the church lets you down.

Or the pastor might. Something Dr. Peter Dogramgi did has always stuck with me. Dr. Dogramgi was my supervising pastor while I was a student at Princeton Seminary. I served for two years as the youth pastor at an ethnic Armenian United Church of Christ congregation just outside of Philadelphia. Dr. Dogramgi was one of the smartest ministers in America. He had a Ph.D. in ethics from Princeton Seminary, and his sermons were hard to comprehend even for a graduate student. When he was done preaching in English, he preached the sermon again, this time in Armenian. It was a wonderful two years, and my wife, Debbie, and I grew to love this congregation and the Dogramgi family. Later Dr. Dogramgi was called to serve the larger UCC denomination as conference minister, and we attended his going-away party at church. During his farewell speech, he told his church, "I know there were times when I let you down as your pastor. I'm sorry. And there were times when you let me down. I forgive you." I will never forget that emotional moment. As I have moved to different ministries, I have always included similar sentiments in final words to the church. Sometimes pastors can let us down.

We can count on the truth not to let us down, right? In the Florida church I served, we had befriended a family whose boys played soccer and Little League baseball with our sons. They started to attend church and they were deciding whether to join. At that time, we were getting ready to celebrate paying off the mortgage and were announcing a mortgage-burning party. The deacons, who were in charge of the event, handed me an announcement to read in church. It was silly, and I blamed it on the deacons. I made a big production of reading it word for word; it read, "What's black and white and red all over? It's not an embarrassed zebra . . . it's the burning of the church mortgage." The family that was considering joining the church thought it was a racial slur and got so mad that they stopped attending.

I called their home, and the mother explained what they thought they had heard. They had to be kidding! I would never say or think anything like that. She did not think I would and thought that is why I read it but blamed it on the deacons. She called our church racist and wondered how I could put up with such a sin. I explained that we were not racist, and I even read the announcement to her over the phone. I still had it. But she insisted that she heard something different and was so upset that she would never forgive the church. We never saw them again. It still troubles me. I assumed that the truth would clarify a misunderstanding. I hoped we could count on the truth to put things right. But, as I discovered that day, sometimes one cannot even depend on truth to make things right.

So what can we depend on in life if we cannot always depend on things, or money or the news, or family or friends, or church or pastors, or even the truth? Is there anything we can count on for sure, no matter what?

In 1609, Dutch explorers came to the New World, to what would become New Amsterdam, and what we know today as New York City. They brought the answer to this question with them, an answer that by this time was nearly fifty years old. Churches in Hungary, Germany, and the Netherlands had already felt the impact of the answer. When Presbyterians arrived in New York, they too embraced the remarkable words of faith that answered life's most important question:

Is there anything we can count on for sure, no matter what?

Zacharias Ursinus, a German Reformer, answered that all-important question in 1563, and he helped the new group of Christians called Protestants understand God's intimate love for them. He penned these words:

Q. What is your only comfort in life and in death?

A. That I belong—body and soul, in life and in death—not to myself but to my faithful Savior, Jesus Christ, who at the cost of his own blood has fully paid for all my sins and has completely freed me from the dominion of the devil; that he protects me so well that without the will of my Father in heaven not a hair can fall from my head; indeed, that everything must fit his purpose for my salvation. [41]

My only comfort in life and in death is "that I belong—body and soul, in life and in death—not to myself but to my faithful Savior, Jesus Christ." When we look over the span of a lifetime, what can be counted on to last? Only one thing—that I belong, body and soul, to my Savior, Jesus.

The apostle Paul said it this way, "For I am convinced that neither death, nor life, nor angels, nor rulers, nor things present, nor things to come, nor powers, nor height, nor depth, nor anything else in all creation, will be able to separate us from the love of God in Christ Jesus our Lord" (Rom. 8:38–39).

That is all we can count on; it is the bottom line. You and I belong, body and soul, to our Savior, Jesus Christ. Our contemporary catechism, *Belonging to God*, offers its answer to that all-important question, "Is there anything we can count on for sure, no matter what?" The contemporary catechism reaches back over 440 years for a satisfying answer. There, in the first question and answer of the Heidelberg Catechism, written by the Reformer Zacharias Ursinus, they found it. Realizing they could not improve upon it, the contemporary writers just paraphr. it for modern ears.

Q. 36. What comfort does the good news give you?

A. 36. That I belong to my faithful Savior Jesus Christ, who died and rose again for my sake, so that nothing will ever separate me from God's love.

As many of you know through your own experience or that of others, the things of this world are not lasting. Health, love, work, financial security, happiness, friendships can let you down—none are guaranteed to last forever. Only one thing lasts; there is only one sure comfort in life and in death: that I belong, body and soul, not to myself, but to my faithful Savior, Jesus Christ. On that, you can hang your hat and your coat and your whole being. Amen.

33
From the Pulpit
2 Timothy 3:16;
Ephesians 6:17; 2 Peter 1:20 – 21

Q. 37. How do we know this good news?
A. 37. Through reading the Bible and hearing it taught and preached. The Holy Spirit inspired those who wrote the Bible, and helps us rely on its promises today.

Our contemporary catechism asks how we know about the good news of God. The answer is short and sweet: through the Bible and through people talking about it. No mysterious midnight visit by an angel is needed. You cannot find out about Jesus by sitting cross-legged on a mountaintop. Tea leaves, zodiac signs, fortune cookies, New Age best-sellers, or neo-psychics will not give you even a clue about the grace-filled, life-altering, excitement-packed, faith-driven gospel of Jesus Christ, the Son of the Living God and our Lord and Savior. For that you have to go to the Bible itself or hear the stories of grace from someone who believes they are true. For the most part, the church is the place where we hear the Bible read from the lectern and the stories of faith told from the pulpit. Week in and week out, God's story is read and preached in hopes that the Holy Spirit of God will energize the words with spiritual power, and that the Spirit will penetrate not only the listener but the speaker as well.

I have a little secret I seldom admit in public. When I preach I am usually talking to myself and if anyone overhears me and finds benefit in the words, then that is gravy. Most people think I am preaching to them. The truth is, I am preaching to Keith Curran. I am wrestling with the grace-filled, life-altering, excitement-packed, faith-driven gospel of Jesus Christ, who is the Son of the Living God and my Lord and Savior. If you could see the wheels turning in my head, you would see them spinning at warp speed as I try to figure out what God has been up to this week in my life and how God's word is speaking to me through the Bible and through the faith stories of those I meet during the week. This may sound selfish or self-centered, but the only way that I know to make the Bible relevant to others is by making it relevant to me. I only hope that the Holy Spirit makes my wrestling match with Scripture, through study and faith, meaningful to you.

Jesus told his disciples to rely on the Holy Spirit to help them understand all the things he did and said. He must have known that it would take thirty years before they would write the stories down so that they looked anything like the Gospels. He must have known that different people would remember things differently and that one person would recall one thing Jesus said or did, while another would recall something different, or see the same thing in a different way. That is human nature and normal. And without the Holy Spirit's help, I am sure we would have had hundreds of Gospels and dozens of stories that, to modern ears, would make no sense at all. The Christian story would have been so convoluted that it would have made no sense. In the canonization process, the early church depended on the guidance of the Holy Spirit to determine what would go into and what would be left out of the New Testament.

It is the Holy Spirit of God, the Spirit of Christ working in the church, which held truths in place and still helps us understand the promises of God. Each Sunday during worship, our liturgist prays the prayer for illumination before the Bible readings, and we ask God's Spirit to help us understand the words and the message. It is helpful to say such a prayer before reading the Bible in devotional time or in church school. The Holy Spirit of God can do wonders for even the most clumsy of readers. The power of the Holy Spirit helps us understand the promises of God in ways that make sense to us, wherever we happen to be on our journey of faith. Amen.

34

The Threefold Action of God

Romans 8:15-16; Acts 1:8; John 15:26-27

Gloria drove up and parked in front of the house. It was November and apple, maple, and oak leaves carpeted the front yard of her childhood home. She watched from her minivan as her father, a retired history professor from the nearby college, used his leaf blower to push the leaves into little piles here and there. Then he would blow the little piles into larger ones. With each merger of leaf piles, he would move to the other side of the lawn and manage the leaves there, then go back to the other side. This autumn dance went on for some time and Gloria watched, undetected. Over the minutes, she noticed that the lawn wasn't getting any cleaner. The leaves were blown around but not piled and bagged. Curiosity held her in her seat. Her father moved one pile closer to another, then blew that one into a thin line and split it with a powerful gust of air from the machine. Into the gap in the line he pushed the larger pile of oak leaves. It overwhelmed the small, broken line of brown and gold maple leaves. Then he moved the other side, pushing that pile back the other way.

Frustrated with her father's progress, Gloria became upset. Why wasn't Dad using the vacuum attachment for the leaf blower she bought him for Father's Day? It had a bag on it and would suck up all the leaves in no time. She watched for a few more minutes as her father rapidly marched a long line of apple tree leaves from the edge of the lawn until they overflowed a number of smaller piles in the middle of the yard. With that, Gloria had had enough. She left the van and walked up the drive. "What are you doing, Dad? I've been watching you for ten minutes and you haven't picked up one single leaf. Why aren't you using the vacuum attachment I got for you?"

"Honey, I loved your gift," he said. "But I don't use it for this."

"How come? It would save you lots of time," she said.

"Sure it would. But that's not the point. You see, being retired, I like to keep my mind fresh. So every October I read all about a historic battle, and when the leaves fall, I reenact the battle in our front yard as I rake the leaves. You've just witnessed Patton's drive across France in 1944."

This story reminds me of Question 38 of the catechism. You may be aware that the world for spirit in both Old and New Testaments is also the word for wind. And like wind, the Spirit of God blows the church into formation to battle the forces of evil and chaos. The Spirit gathers us here each week, strengthens our ranks, fortifies our defenses, and moves us into position to be God's people at a strategic moment and for a specific situation. The Spirit of God, as God's active effort in life, readies and positions us. Then God's Spirit sends us into the fray, empowered and enforced so that the gospel can be proclaimed and justice and mercy can be won.

Q. 38. What else does the Holy Spirit do for the church?

A. 38. The Spirit gathers us to worship God, builds us up in faith, hope, and love, and sends us into the world to proclaim the gospel and to work for justice and peace.

You can hear the threefold action of God's Spirit in this: **gathers, builds up, and sends out the church.**

First, the Spirit of God gathers us for worship. I just returned from a week of study at Columbia Seminary in Georgia. Outside, the much-needed rain muddied up the campus, but inside a dozen Presbyterian pastors studied with Professor Brian Wren, renowned hymn writer and author of eleven hymns in our *Presbyterian Hymnal.* The focus of our work was to make prayers for worship more meaningful and Spirit-directed. Dr. Wren gave us much to think about in class and lots of homework. Our assignment was to create well-prepared, heart-centered prayers with rhythm, imagery, and theologically sound content.

Dr. Wren pointed out that many churches continue to err in their worship services. The service begins with an invocation, a prayer that invokes God to be present in their midst. When you think about it, you can see the problem. In the Directory of Worship, an opening prayer, a prayer of confession, and a seasonal prayer are suggested, but an invocation is not. Why?

God is here already! There is no need to invoke the presence of God if God is already present! Jesus said when two or three are gathered in his name, he is there with them in Spirit (see Matt. 18:19). Whenever you are with another Christian, Christ is with you and it can be a worshipful moment. When you are alone, Christ is with you as well. He also promised to be Emmanuel, God with us. The Spirit gathers us into community, and the Spirit is waiting for us when we are in the assembly.

What does that look like? Kierkegaard may have described it best with his famous illustration of worship. Worship is like a play. In a play, those on stage are the actors. A director is in the wings and those in the auditorium are the audience enjoying the show. That is how it is in the theater and, sadly, how some churches view worship. But in this Sabbath play, the minister is the director, the congregation is on stage as the actors, and God is the one in the audience, enjoying the praise and adoration. In a theater, can you imagine the curtain rising and the actors calling to those on the street to come and watch? No, the audience is already there before the curtain goes up. In church, the audience is God. Can you picture that? Can you see yourself as an actor in the worship service?

Second, the Spirit of God builds us up in faith, hope, and love. "O Lord, if there is a Lord, save my soul, if I have a soul. . . ." A prayer such as this would have gotten high marks in Professor Wren's class. At least it is honest, which is the most important thing about a prayer. Is it real? Sometimes a prayer like this is the best one can do. It reminds me of the apostle Thomas, perhaps the easiest disciple for us to identify with. Thomas wanted to look at the evidence, and Jesus was more than willing to show it to him. The nail holes in his hands and feet and the slash in his side were more than enough evidence for Thomas to believe. The Holy Spirit is more than willing to show us that God's Spirit can be believed.

The Spirit of God builds up our hope as well as our love. When the New Testament was written, the writers had a choice of which word to use to express love. In English we are limited to basically one word and we add meaning to that word by its context. In Greek, the word could be *eros* or *philia* or *agape*. *Eros,* sensual love, is all "take"; *philia,* friendly love, is "give and take"; *agape,* unconditional love, is all "give." *Agape* is the love that God's Spirit builds up in us. It is a love that gives, even at the risk of giving it all away.

There is an ancient Gaelic legend that tells of an eagle that swoops down and grabs a small child and takes it up to its mountain eyrie. The strong men of the village attempt to climb the steep rock face to retrieve the child, but fail. Suddenly, past them climbs a slender woman. With every ounce of her being, she reaches the top and rescues the child. "How did you do that?" the strong men ask. The answer: "I am the baby's mother." Her love enabled her to outdistance the strongest. So does our love when God's Spirit enables it.

Third, God's Spirit sends out the church to share the gospel, which must include Christ's message of justice and peace.

The world's best answer to one of the most asked questions is found in the brief Old Testament book of Micah. It is dedication day, the time when worshipers brought their tithes and offerings to the Temple. Much like in a contemporary church on Stewardship Sunday, many asked, "What shall I bring to the House of the Lord?" (Mic. 6:6, paraphr.) and "What does the Lord require of me?" (see Mic. 6:8). To this all-important question came the world's best answer: **to do justice, love mercy, and walk humbly with your God** (Mic. 6:8). God not only cares about our offerings, but God cares even more about our attitude and how we live for God each day.

Injustice is happening all around us. A neglected child, an unfair promotion, a repair rip-off, a lie taken as a truth, cheating on a test, an unfaithful spouse, corporate greed, and lottery ads geared to those who can least afford to gamble their money away are just not right. It is like a poor man asking a millionaire how many more dollars it would take to satisfy him, as the millionaire reaches into the poor man's pocket and says, "Just one more." Injustice is everywhere, but the Holy Spirit sends the church out into the world to offer the gospel of Jesus Christ as an alternative value system in a materialistic society. It is a challenge that can be so frightening that many retreat into thinking only of themselves. But for others, the challenge is a clarion call to find ways to offer self in Christ's name.

Many veterans know this kind of sacrificial value system. Our nation honors the brave with holidays like Veterans Day and Memorial Day. Their spirited sacrifice in war may have reflected the Holy Spirit's presence. Many will swear it did. A young girl at church gave all her birthday money away to the Cancer Society to help find a cure for a disease. She was Spirit-guided. Often such challenges bring out the best in people. As Robert Kennedy said, each time we stand for an ideal, or act to improve the lot of others, or strike out against injustice, we send forth a tiny ripple of hope in this world. His challenge sounds much like a call to join the Holy Spirit in its work. The Holy Spirit sends us out to do what is just, to love mercy, and to live in humble fellowship with our God and each other. Let the Holy Spirit send you out to the people, places, and situations where you can share the gospel of peace and justice in the week ahead. Amen.

35
Lord's Day Worship
Luke 24:1-2; Acts 20:7

O ur tour bus jerked to a halt. The driver waved his arms windmill-style, and John, our tour guide, yelled in Arabic what we hoped would be kind words of encouragement to the mass of Palestinian women and children that flooded the road, sidewalk, and alleyways on all sides of our bus. Bethlehem was our destination, but Manger Square, Shepherds' Hill, and the much anticipated gift shop would just have to wait. The human mass paid no attention to the diesel horn or our driver's animated dance from the driver's seat. He inched the bus forward, and in response to the motion of the huge, blue Mercedes bus, the mass became still. Our driver pulled ahead as an opening appeared. The racket from hundreds of voices split in half as the bus picked up speed and moved through the opening. Then *screech!* The brakes yelled as the bus lurched to a stop. Those who had window seats saw what happened. As the bus picked up speed, an elderly woman darted out, stopped and saw the oncoming bus. She tried to race to the other side. The bumper of the bus brushed her flowing dress as she landed on the curb just in the nick of time. A close call.

"Why would she do that?" we all asked at once. Where was everyone going in such a rush? It was Thursday afternoon yet it looked like a holiday. Why all the pushing and shoving? What was so important to make her do that? Our questions kept coming. Our guide explained that it was the Muslim day of worship. They were on their way to the mosque and *nothing*, not even a big tour bus filled with Americans, was going to get in the way of their day of worship.

Studies indicate that Americans are not that excited about going to church. About 45 percent of people say they attend church each week, but other studies prove that it is more like 25 percent who actually attend worship on any given Sunday.

Muslims worship on the sixth day of the week, and Jews worship on the seventh, while Christians worship on the first, on Sunday. Our contemporary catechism explains:

Q. 39. Why do Christians gather for worship on the first day of the week?

A. 39. Because it is the day when God raised our Lord Jesus from the dead. When we gather weekly on that day, the Spirit makes our hearts glad with the memory of our Lord's resurrection.

In Old Testament times, the day of worship was the seventh day of the week, the day God rested from the work of creation. It is the day marked in the Ten Commandments as the Sabbath, when there could be no work or play. The people rested from their labors. The concept of no work or play on the Sabbath carried over to the Protestant Church at the Reformation and was made into a strict principle by the Puritans, Anabaptists, and Calvinists of Europe. That strict Sabbath ethic carried into the mid-1950s for American Protestantism and eventually weakened when the 1960s came around.

Because I grew up Roman Catholic, I had almost no Sabbath ethic and I was always comfortable doing just about anything that I wanted on a Sunday. While serving my first church just out of seminary, I learned quickly that in some communities there still were strict expectations about work on the Sabbath.

It was a spring day. I had led worship at both congregations I served, and I was relaxing. The manse was on the town's only street. The house had just been re-sided with blue vinyl so I thought I would spruce up the front and paint the two front doors with white paint. It was a great day to paint and not too cold to take the doors off their hinges and prop them up on the front porch. A few days later, some older members of the church quizzed me about painting the doors. I explained that I bought the paint myself and wanted to keep up the house as my donation to the manse effort. That was not their concern, of course. They wondered why their minister was working on the Sabbath.

For the most part, the traditional Sabbath culture in America has disappeared. Soccer games, Jiffy Lube, Home Depot, the movies, lawn mowing, and office hours have become the norm for Sundays. Sundays for Christians have become as secular as the workweek. In fact, Sunday is now considered by many in corporate America a part of the workweek.

How many remember the blue laws? Those born after 1965 or so have no memory of them. Blue laws were state and local government-imposed restrictions on doing business on the Christian Sabbath. Some sociologists believe that taking the blue laws off the books marked the official beginning of the post-Christian age.

For four thousand years, the Sabbath has been a day of rest for Israel. It was designed to be a time of spiritual renewal and reflection on God's graciousness. Regular Sabbath observance for the Jews outwardly demonstrated an internal trust in the Lord that allowed them to let go of providing for themselves one day each week. This was very much a sacramental act, a spiritual drama acted out every seven days. "God will provide. It is not all up to me."

For Christians, there is not the obligation to follow the strict Sabbath laws of the Torah. Jesus freed us from the Law, yet the admonition of the Ten Commandments to keep the Sabbath holy remains with us still. While honoring the commandment, the church also honors its Lord and Savior. The day of resurrection is the Lord's Day, the appropriate time to worship Jesus Christ.

Our text from Acts 20 marks the first instance that Sunday worship is recorded in the Bible. The church gathered on the first day of the week to break bread and share the Word of God. The New Testament breaking of bread refers to the Lord's Supper. As the new church gathered, they heard the Word of God proclaimed in preaching. On the first day of the week, Christians came together to call on God in the name of Jesus of Nazareth. A shift had taken place. The Fourth Commandment had been reworked and reinvented for a new day. The empty tomb changed everything.

First-day worship was in fact a "little Easter." Every Sunday is a day of resurrection in miniature. When we gather to offer praise and prayer in the name of the one who rose on a Sunday, we acknowledge Easter's reality. The empty tomb changed everything, even our day of worship.

I once heard that the spiritual practice of worshiping week after week is like the process of refining precious metal. A Hebrew text says, "God will sit as a refiner and purifier of silver" (Mal. 3:3). To refine silver, the silversmith grabs a piece of the raw metal and holds it over the flame. As it heats up, the silversmith must hold it in the middle of the flame, the hottest part. There the heat burns away the impurities. Sometimes when we are in worship, we may wonder why God lets us sit in the hot spots for a time. It may be helpful to remember that God sits as a refiner and purifier of silver.

The silversmith sits in front of the fire the whole time the silver is being refined. The silversmith not only has to remain at the furnace, but also has to keep a constant eye on the metal. If the silver is left just a moment too long in the flame, there is a chance it could be destroyed. Sometimes as we worship, we may wonder if God is still interested in us. It may be helpful to remember that God sits as a refiner and purifier of silver, keeping hold of you, keeping his eye on you and never turning away lest anything harm you.

Like all artists, silversmiths work not from rote but by intuition and feel. They know the silver is fully refined when they can see their image in it. If you feel the heat in worship sometimes, it may be helpful to remember that God has a tight grip on you. God keeps an eye on you, never looking away. God is an artist and will work your life until God's very image is seen in you.

Amen.

36

Ready, Set, WORSHIP!

Ephesians 5:19-20; Psalm 92:1-4

Ready, set, WORSHIP! Come on. Let's go! Hop to it! Put your knees into it. Lift those voices. Sing those hymns. I can't hear yoooou!"

Can you imagine your minister as a drill sergeant and worship as a boot camp? We would worship and we would worship RIGHT! "Get down and give me twelve Apostles' Creeds." Worshiping "right" looks nothing like the results a drill sergeant could get from us, however. In fact, worshiping right has little to do with our ability and everything to do with the graciousness of God. Yet it is important to worship well, in a fashion that brings honor to God and with beliefs that are based on sound theology. Our contemporary catechism helps us to understand what constitutes right worship.

Q. 40. What do we do in Christian worship?

A. 40. We adore and praise God. We pray, sing hymns, and listen to readings from the Bible. We also give offerings to God for the work of the church, and commit ourselves to serve God and our neighbors. Above all, we hear the preaching of the gospel and celebrate the sacraments.

You will see in our church bulletin the order of our worship service. The five-point outline puts Question 40 into practice. All the elements of appropriate worship are there: praise, prayers, music, Scripture, offering of gifts and self, preaching, and the sacraments of baptism and the Lord's Supper (when observed). They are all included in our outline of worship, an outline that has been the basic structure for Christian worship for much of history.

The question remains, however: How do we begin worship? We can't just start with "ready, set, WORSHIP!" Like a public school teacher, I know the futility of rapping on the desk and calling, "Pay attention, please." True attention takes some intentionality. It takes some effort to ready ourselves for God to encounter us in worship. In the monastery, monks have a practice they call *statio*, which means stopping one thing before beginning another. The time between activities gives them a moment to pause and reflect on what just ended and what is to come next.

Similarly, rather than rushing in and worshiping God, we take a few moments for *statio*. The organ music helps to make the transition from world to worship. The prelude makes us aware of the in-between time. The Quakers called this a time for centering the self. In our worship service we begin by taking our seats, settling down, listening to the organ voluntary, and looking to the cross. This part of the service is called **Preparing to worship.** This is the point at which our expectations rise. We hope that worship will leave us in a different spiritual and mental state than when we arrived. In the *statio* moment between the world and worship, we ready ourselves to be changed by the God who draws us near.

The choir or the pastor—or both—will call us to worship the Lord, who deserves every ounce of praise we feeble human beings can muster. We sing expressions of faith that lift up the qualities of our God through the blending of music and poetry and psalms. Scripture tells us to sing hymns and spiritual songs (Eph. 5:19). Human beings are the subjects of spiritual songs, but God is the subject of hymns. "A Mighty Fortress Is Our God" is a hymn. When we sing "I Saw the Light, I Saw the Light" or "I've Got Peace Like a River" we are singing spiritual songs. Either way, we are praising God. This portion of worship is called **Praise to God.**

You may wonder why the confession of sin is in this section. It is a logical move from praising the Almighty, Eternal, All Knowing, All Loving God and Creator of all that is seen and unseen, to realizing who and what we are in comparison with our Holy God. We see God and then realize how broken and shallow we human beings really are. We cannot help falling to our knees in humble reverence. When the prophet Isaiah was drawn into God's presence, his first instinct was to turn away, saying, "It is hopeless for me. I'm doomed. Anything I can say sounds stupid, because I'm just a human being" (Isa. 6:5, paraphr.). And as Isaiah learned, our confession of sin brings with it the promise that God will enfold us in grace and forgiveness. We praise God even more! As we sing the words of the ancient Gloria Patri praising God the Father, Son, and Holy Ghost, we move to the next phase of worship: **The Word read and proclaimed.**

I have been reading the theology of Karl Barth recently. In seminary I studied his monumental work, *Church Dogmatics*. Barth influenced much of twentieth-century Christianity and especially American Presbyterianism. The Confession of 1967 expresses Barthian theology. Writing and teaching during the early and middle part of his century, Barth helped refocus Protestant theology away from what we can know about God in our own minds to what God has revealed to humankind in Jesus Christ. This was a dramatic redefinition of theology for the time, and Barth's influence remains strong today. Our contemporary catechism bubbles with Barthian theology.

I bring up Barth because I recently had one of those "Aha!" moments. It answered a question that I did not know needed asking. Why do we keep reading Scripture and preaching about our faith? Why do we keep bothering to learn about living the Christian life if we are already saved? Why do we want to know more if we already have faith? In other words, why do we put such a high priority on the sermon in worship? As the preacher who puts ten to fifteen hours a week into this particular task, I would like to know!

From his study of Anselm's *Proof for the Existence of God* in 1931, Barth realized that we have a drive for meaning and understanding that proceeds from our faith. Anselm held that faith seeks understanding because this is a characteristic of Christian faith, and he restated it as a motto: *I believe in order that I might understand.* It is faith itself that summons us to knowledge.[42] Barth goes on to say that, as its result, our search for meaning in Scripture leads to faith. This is the meaning of the phrase "from faith to faith." Our faith generates a desire for understanding, and our learning leads to a richer faith. From faith to faith.

The Scriptures are the highest expressions of the church's faith. To find a saving knowledge of Jesus Christ and meaning to life, we have to read the Scriptures and hear them interpreted in the sermon. One hearing is not enough to relieve our Christian hunger for God's grace or to satisfy our unquenchable thirst for meaning. So in worship we read Scripture and hear sermons because we just cannot do without them.

Our Response to the Gospel is with acts of faith. We sing, we make a profession of faith, we pray, we ordain and confirm, we offer our gifts, we break bread at the Table, we commission work camp youth, we meditate, pass the peace of Christ, light candles, anoint with oil, and hear our friends share their joys and concerns.

The closing phase of worship is called **Departure to serve God.** Some have called it the "so what" phase. Others have called it the "now what" phase. And some have called it the "Who, me?" phase. Yet others have been known to call it the "Why me?" phase. We remember our hopes at the start of the service to rise up from hearing the Word in a different state than that in which we sat down. And if we have been willing to meet God halfway, then that promise is kept.

The apostle Paul spells out what he hopes we find in right worship. "Set your minds on what the Spirit desires," he says to the Roman church (Rom. 12:2, paraphr.). He writes to the people of the Philippian church that he hopes they will come away from worship thinking new thoughts: "Finally, beloved, whatever is true, whatever is noble, whatever is right, whatever is pure, whatever is lovely, whatever is admirable, if any things are excellent or praiseworthy—think on these" (Phil. 4:8, paraphr.). With the benediction, we are challenged and blessed. The benediction also answers the great question "Whom shall I send?" If we are attentive and brave, we can humbly answer, "Here I am; send me." Amen.

37
A Visible Sign of Invisible Grace
Mark 1:9-11, 14:22-25

The contemporary catechism covers a wide array of topics, including creation, grace, the life and work of Jesus, the Spirit of God, the Bible, ethics, and the work of the church. The sacraments are central to the Christian faith, and they symbolize the deepest connection of Christ to Christ's body—the Christian community of faith, or the church.

Q. 41. What is a sacrament?

A. 41. A sacrament is a special act of Christian worship that uses visible signs to present God's grace for us in Jesus Christ. We believe that two sacraments were given by Jesus: baptism and the Lord's Supper.

The two Scripture readings from Mark's Gospel provide background on the two sacraments that Jesus commissioned for the church. The word *sacrament* does not appear in the Bible. *Sacrament* describes a sacred action practiced by the church that conveys a sense of God's love for believers. The word comes from the Latin word for pledge, although it may be more closely connected with the New Testament Latin word *mysterion,* meaning "a sacred mystery." How pouring water over a baby's head or eating a bite of bread and an ounce of grape juice or wine can have spiritual value remains just as much of a mystery to us in the twenty-first century as in other eras of Christendom. We do these things and trust that they have spiritual value because Jesus commended them to us. Two thousand years of Christianity have proved beyond doubt that when the church acts out the sacraments, human lives change for the better.

A classical definition of a sacrament is: an outward and visible sign of an inward and spiritual grace. Augustine defined it as a visible sign of an invisible reality. According to our contemporary catechism: **A sacrament is a special act of Christian worship that uses visible signs to present God's grace for us in Jesus Christ.**

In the twelfth century, the church had over thirty sacramental actions. Theologian Peter Lombard refined the number to seven.[43] The Roman Catholic Church still holds to that number. In the Protestant Reformation, the Reformers returned to the Bible and found that the early church established two sacred actions: baptism and the Lord's Supper. Both were actions that Jesus told us to do. Protestant churches today still hold that there are two sacraments. They call the other sacred actions of the church "ordinances." Ordination and marriage, for example, are church ordinances. Although they are not sacraments, they are visible signs, revealed in covenantal promises and the laying on of hands, of what God is doing in the lives of Christians. A sacrament is a mystery! We cannot fully understand it and it always will puzzle us.

The great Norwegian explorer Roald Amundsen was the first to discover the magnetic meridian of the North Pole and the first to go to the South Pole. On one of his expeditions, Amundsen took a homing pigeon with him. When he had finally reached the top of the world, he opened the bird's cage and set it free. Back in Norway, his wife looked up and saw the pigeon circling their home. Imagine the rush of emotion when she saw this sign indicating that her husband was all right and had reached the pole! The pigeon gave her proof that her husband was alive. It was a visible sign of something she could not see happening. But it was enough for her to know that he was on his way home.

The water, the bread, and the cup are visible signs of something we cannot see, but we trust they are enough for us to know that God is at work, that grace and love are alive and very much present. We may not be able to see it, but the drama of water and the table remind us again and again that God's invisible grace is coming to us where we need it the most.

Thanks be to God!

38

Ready for a New Life

Matthew 28:16–20; Galatians 3:27–28

Have you ever heard of a mystery within a mystery? In the movie *The Sixth Sense* the audience gets involved with a story about a child psychologist who tries to help a little boy who says he sees dead people. According to the little boy, the dead people use him to fix problems left undone at the time of their death. The psychologist himself is caught up in his own broken life and intense sadness. But the psychologist is the only one who is able to have an impact on the troubled child. Trust is created as they communicate. The boy seems to be getting the help he needs, and this positive therapy is the only thing in the psychologist's life that seems to be going right. But through it all, the audience always senses that there is something strange going on. There is a mysterious quality to the story, which piques the audience's sense of comfort. *Suddenly* . . . the mystery is revealed! An audible "Oh!" ripples through the audience, who discern that the story is really a mystery within a mystery, one about the boy and another one about the psychologist.

The movie helps put baptism in perspective. Just as the movie reveals a mystery within a mystery, so it is with the sacrament of baptism. The word *sacrament* means sacred mystery. We cannot fully understand how God works through simple earthly actions like water poured or bread broken. It will puzzle us, and puzzle us, and puzzle us until Christ returns. We will never get our mental arms around the whole thing. God said "Do it," yet it remains a sacred mystery in the church.

Our contemporary catechism highlights the mystery within the mystery of the sacrament of baptism by calling on the triune God, the three natures of our God, Father, Son, and Spirit. This is a theological mystery within a sacred mystery but some aspects of baptism are more accessible to us.

Q. 42. What is baptism?

A. 42. Through baptism I am adopted and welcomed into God's family. In the water of baptism I share in the dying and rising of Jesus, who washes away my sins. I am made one with him, and with all who are joined to him in the church.

Q. 43. Why are you baptized in the name of the Father, and of the Son, and of the Holy Spirit?

A. 43. Because of the command Jesus gave to his disciples. After he was raised from the dead, he appeared to them, saying, "Go . . . and make disciples of all nations, baptizing them in the name of the Father and of the Son and of the Holy Spirit."

Q. 44. What is the meaning of this name?

A. 44. It is the name of the Holy Trinity. The Father is God, the Son is God, and the Holy Spirit is God. And yet they are not three gods, but one God in three persons. We worship God in this mystery.

There is a lot we do not know about baptism, although we can speak symbolically of four actions that the waters of baptism signify.

Adoption, dying and rising, cleansing, and joining are activities that happen at the spiritual level as we enact them in the sacrament. What we do on the outside exemplifies what God is doing for the believer on the inside.

Dr. Laura Schlessinger, the radio therapist, was counseling a teenage girl who was searching for her birth father. The birth father had abandoned the family before the girl was born. The girl desired to make a connection but was unable to do so because the father had severed all ties with his past. She asked Dr. Laura if she should keep trying.

Pointing out that her adoptive father had married her mother and adopted and raised her since she was an infant, Dr. Laura asked the girl to speculate about his feelings. The girl replied, "He must feel really hurt that I'm more interested in a man I never met than I am in him." Dr. Laura asked if her adoptive father loved her. "Oh, yes. He loves me very much." Dr. Laura then asked, "Why are you hurting your adoptive father so much?" The girl could not answer. Dr. Laura then said, "He is the one who freely chose to love you with his whole heart. He wasn't forced into it. You weren't an accident he had to live with nor a bit of bad luck he was saddled with. He freely chose to love you and care for you. He is your 'real' father!"

Baptism is an adoption into the family of God. We are not born into the faith, but God does everything to make us his children. And when we place ourselves under the waters of baptism, we let God choose us because we know that God really loves us. He is our "real" heavenly Father and our loving God. In baptism, we enter a family populated with other adopted children, and our children are offered the same promise that was offered to us.

In the book of Acts we read: "For the promise is for you, for your children, and for all who are far away, everyone whom the Lord our God calls to him" (Acts 2:39). The drama of baptism takes us into, under, and through biblical waters. The crossing of the Red Sea, boating on the Sea of Galilee, John preaching in the River Jordan, the baptism of Jesus, the woman's discovery of living water at Jacob's Well, and the flowing forth of water from Christ's pierced heart on the cross are all reenacted when we gather at the font.

The *three-peat* of water over our heads is striking. Three times the water is brought over the head—in the name of the Father, Son, and Holy Spirit. Three times underwater is reminiscent of the three days that Jesus was under the ground. On the third day he rose again to new life. The third time we come up out of the water, we are people with new life. In baptism we die and are raised with Christ. Paul wrote to the Roman Christians: "Don't you know that when baptized we share his death? We're buried with him by baptism so that, just like Christ, we can be raised from the dead so that we can walk in the newness of life" (Rom. 6:3–4, paraphr.).

A debate still rages over the fact that there are two Gospel accounts of Jesus' own baptism by John the Baptist. The language of Mark, the first Gospel to be written, tells us that Jesus came up out of the water after being baptized by John. The Greek can be translated to mean either that Jesus came up from the water after being fully immersed in it or that Jesus came up from and out of the river to dry land after John had poured water over his head (Presbyterian sprinkling). Either rendering is possible from the text as it is written.

There is an old joke about a Presbyterian minister who debated a Baptist pastor, asking, "Is baptism legitimate if a person is only wet up to his knees?" "No. That doesn't count!" the Baptist said. "How about if a person is wet up to his waist?" the Presbyterian asked. "No." "How about if he gets wet up to his shoulders?" "No, that doesn't count. You have to have the water over the head," the Baptist pastor insisted.

"So it doesn't count if the water is over your knees or waist or shoulders. It only counts if the water is over your head. Well, that's exactly what we do; we put the water over the head!" The Baptist pastor walked away scratching his head and murmuring, "He got me on that, but somehow it just doesn't seem right!"

On the other hand, there is the story about a hardheaded preacher who loved to preach that baptism did not count unless you are completely immersed. Almost every time he preached, he preached on full-immersion baptism and contended that any other way was wrong. His sermons became boring, and the deacons of the church approached the preacher and reminded him that many old-time preachers would pick their sermons by letting the Spirit inspire the text. They would let the Bible fall open at random and then preach on whatever text they saw first. The preacher liked the idea and tried it the next Sunday.

When it came time to preach he let his Bible fall open. He stuck his finger on the page and, misreading the word *turtledove,* read the text: "And the voice of the turtle was heard in the land" (Song of Solomon 2:12). And straightaway, he began to preach.

"Oh bretheren and sisteren, this mornin' as I was a-heading to church, I had to cross the bridge over the creek back yonder. The sun was shinin' down on the rocks there, and the mud turtles was a-sunning theirselves on them rocks. I stopped for a minute on yon side to watch them, but when I started acrost that there bridge, them turtles went into the water *kerplunk!* Now bretheren and sisteren, they didn't reach down there and get a little water and sprinkle on their heads. No, and they didn't just go halfway into the water. No, when they went in they went all the way in. And there, bretheren and sisteren, your have your doctrine of total immersion!" [44]

Full immersion or sprinkling—either way, the water cannot actually wash away any sins. That happens on the inside and is done by God through grace and love because of the cross. What we do on the outside only hints at what God is doing on the inside. No soap, however pure, can wash away our sins. Only God can do that, but it happens on the inside.

Adoption, dying and rising, cleansing and joining are activities that happen on the spiritual level in baptism. We are made one with Jesus and one with each other in baptism. Paul says that this is like a wrecking ball that blasts away the barriers that once separated people: "As many of you as were baptized into Christ have clothed yourselves with Christ. There is no longer Jew or Greek, there is no longer slave or free, there is no longer male or female, for all of you are one in Christ Jesus" (Gal. 3:27–28).

Another time he said, "For just as the body is one and has many members, and all the members of the body, though many, are one body, so it is with Christ. For in the one Spirit we were all baptized into one body—Jews or Greeks, slaves or free—and we were all made to drink of one Spirit" (1 Cor. 12:12–13). God is faithful in the promise to make us one with Jesus and one with each other. As it says in the hymn, "There is no shadow of turning with Thee."[45] God's promise is for today and tomorrow, and it is a promise that is not going to fail.

God has chosen us for inclusion in God's family. We have new life. Our sins are forgiven. And we are Christ's siblings and true friends of one another. Baptism is like getting four blessings in one; a family, a new life, forgiveness, and the presence of Jesus Christ.

"Blessings all mine, with ten thousand beside!" [46]

Prayer: Precious Jesus, our Savior, of the many wonders of your world, these three words tell so much about you: washing, sanctifying, and justifying. And we have experienced all of them firsthand in baptism. You washed us clean, acquitted us of all crimes. Unstained! Unpolluted! And, as if that weren't enough, you made us members of your family. You freely gave us what we could not give ourselves—a new life, a name that marks us as your people. Amen.

39

Feeding on Jesus' Love

1 Corinthians 10:16; 11:23-26

S ometimes I *think* that I have come up with a brand new idea. One time, when the Pittsburgh Steelers football team was on a roll and heading for the playoffs, everyone in western Pennsylvania was trying to come up with a new nickname for the Steelers' powerful defense. It had to match— or at least come close to—the nickname of the past Super Bowl champion team, the Steel Curtain. The newspaper held a contest and asked readers to submit suggestions. Mine was the "Blitzburgh Steelers," because that year the defense was really fast and loved to blitz. Lo and behold—"Blitzburgh" was chosen as the best nickname! Banners with "Blitzburgh" hung all around downtown Pittsburgh. Shirts shouted "Blitzburgh!" Billboards, television news, advertisements on city buses: "Blitzburgh!" My family could not live with me. I kept bragging that I had made up the name. They kept saying that I was nuts. They didn't believe I came up with it all by myself.

I got a call from the local newspaper wondering if I was, in fact, the one who had come up with the name. I explained that I had submitted it. The newspaper wanted to do a story on me, but I told the reporter that I first wanted to do some of my own research on the contest. I went to the public library and went through old newspapers to find the contest details and to see if I had won a prize. And there, to my dismay, I discovered that my family was right. I *was* nuts. I remember coming up with the name "Blitzburgh" all on my own and writing it down on the contest form. But there on the form, in small print, which I did not see at the time, were instructions and some suggested nicknames, including . . . "Blitzburgh"! Someone else had come up with the idea first!

I tell you this story because I am sure that someone has already written a book or doctoral dissertation on the following idea. However, it is a new thought for me. I have never heard anyone else even suggest it. I am cautiously claiming it as a new idea. Have you ever made the connection between Jesus' birth and the Lord's Supper? Jesus was born and Mary made a bed for him in a crib converted from a cattle-feeding bin called a manger. Jesus was gently placed in a manger, just as cattle food would be placed there. Jesus' first contact with the world of flesh and blood was in a feeding trough, where food is offered. Can this be only a coincidence? Could it not be an intentional foreshadowing of the Lord's Supper? Is it at all interesting to you that the babe in a manger became the man called the Bread of Life? Isn't it interesting that his first contact on earth was in a feeding trough? Is it possible that God was trying to tell us something back then in Bethlehem about his intention for his Son in Jerusalem? Is it not possible that the manger story foreshadows the message of the Lord's Supper?

Jesus took the bread, and when he had given thanks, he broke it and said, "This is my body that is for you. Do this in remembrance of me" (1 Cor. 11:23–24). We are to feed on Jesus' love. At Communion, we feed on Jesus' love. We break bread, share it, and eat it. As we consider the sacrament of the Lord's Supper, instead of looking for a new revelation, it may be best to hear a time-tested and theologically approved explanation. We have to look no farther than our contemporary catechism.

Q. 45. What is the Lord's Supper?

A. 45. In the Lord's Supper I am fed at the table of God's family. Through the bread that I eat and the cup that I drink, the Lord offers me his body and blood. He renews my faith, and gives me the gift of eternal life. As I remember that he died for all, and therefore also for me, I feed on him in my heart by faith with thanksgiving.

Just as baptism is a sacred mystery, so is Holy Communion. We act out a God-initiated and time-tested drama that demonstrates what is happening on the inside at the spiritual level. When we break the bread we remember that Jesus' own body was broken so that we can be whole. When we share the bread, we demonstrate the Christian calling to share what is most important in our lives with others. What is more important than Jesus' love? When we eat the bread, we physically demonstrate that we find nourishment in the bread, showing that as we feed on Christ's love, our spirits are nourished.

When we pour the cup, we try to conceptualize life's most meaningful sacrifice: "This is my blood," Jesus said. When we pass the cup, are we not sharing the same blessing, which makes us one in Christ? When we drink the cup, we are internalizing the outcome of the sacrifice—we are made right with God by grace through Christ. When we drink the cup together, we are saying that we all need the grace being offered us; we all have fallen short of the glory of God and stand in need of forgiveness and new life.

When we finish and offer the peace of Christ to those around us, can you see in that outward action that the inner blessing is validated? Yes, what we do on the outside points to what is happening on the inside. But more than mystery is active at the table. The apostle Paul, in writing to the Corinthian Christians, refreshes their memories by letting them know what he has remembered about Communion.

Jesus of Nazareth said, "Do this in remembrance of me'" (Luke 22:19b). Paul said, "For I received from the Lord what I also handed on to you, that the Lord Jesus on the night when he was betrayed took a loaf of bread, and when he had given thanks, he broke it and said, 'This is my body that is for you. Do this in remembrance of me' " (1 Cor. 11:23–24). I've remembered this and I pass it on to you to remember. Paul again says, "For as often as you eat this bread and drink the cup, you proclaim the Lord's death until he comes" (1 Cor. 11:26). At Communion, we remember Jesus until he comes again. With so much remembering going on, I can safely say the Lord's Supper must be about remembering!

As we feed on Jesus' love, we are nourished and fortified to share that love with everyone we meet. That's how people know we are his disciples. That's how people can tell we are part of the body of Christ in and for the world.

40

Prayer, Part 1

Romans 8:26-27; Psalm 38:9, 42:1

D o you ever wonder if God can hear you when you pray? No matter where you are, even when your prayers are only a whisper, God hears you. Even when you do not know what to say to God, your prayers get through.

Q. 46. Why do we pray to God?

A. 46. Because we are created to live with God, who desires the prayers of our hearts. Our hearts long for God, for we need God's help and guidance every day.

The contemporary Presbyterian catechism, *Belonging to God*, explores prayer in the next few questions and answers. First generally, and then specifically, the why and how of prayer are addressed. Then the catechism walks us through the Lord's Prayer, phrase by phrase.

As I see it, prayer is a multifaceted experience that is real and trustworthy. **Prayer is God communicating with us.** Prayer is God speaking to us through Scripture when we open ourselves to such a transcendent experience. God speaks to our church every Sunday through Scripture, if we let this happen. When God calls us beloved, God is talking directly to you and to me. And although we read the same words, God may say something unique to each of us. It may even happen today.

Prayer allows God to communicate to us through experiences like coincidences. Someone once said that a coincidence is a miracle in which God wants to remain anonymous. Sometimes we can sense God's direction, God's hand in our lives through our experiences. When one door closes, look for a window to open.

One Bible study about King David focused on his introduction to King Saul. Saul was having night terrors. Nothing could calm him down except music. Someone suggested that David, a young man who played the harp and sang godly songs, might be the answer to Saul's disquieted spirit. David played when Saul awoke and gently sang him back to sleep like a mother singing a lullaby to a baby. Was it just chance that David found his way into the king's court? Or was it God working through David's experiences, communicating God's direction for his life?

Prayer is God communicating with us through a fleece. You may remember the story of Gideon, one of the Hebrew judges who ruled Israel before King Saul's time. One time he prayed that God would give him an answer. He asked God to show him the right thing to do. Gideon put a woolen fleece on the ground and said to God, "If it is dry in the morning when the rest of the ground is wet from dew, then I will know the answer." In the morning, the fleece was dry (Judg. 6:36–40, paraphr.). For me, that would have been sign enough. But Gideon did it again, just to make sure. Of course, God gave him the same answer. God communicates with us through the fleece we set down.

God communicates with us through our intuition. Even when we do not get a yes or a no or a maybe, we can often tell when God is saying something to us. But be careful with this. The purpose of prayer is not to make us feel good—an honest encounter with God may not produce this result at all! The intention behind true prayer is to be changed in a way that contributes to God's ongoing transformation in the world.

Prayer is also talking to God. Much of the time, folks in the congregation I serve do not have any trouble talking to God. In fact, we would be happy if we could do ALL the talking and God all the listening. Now, this seems to be not only the preference of St. Andrew folks, but that of all humanity. Sometimes, however, we find ourselves speechless: on our knees, without words on our tongues.

The apostle Paul said, "At times like that, don't worry. The Holy Spirit will do our praying for us" (Rom. 8:26, paraphr.). When words do not or cannot come, let go and let the Spirit pray for you. It is said that the moment you surrender yourself to God, you are surrendering to an unknown future and destiny. You are letting yourself become the person whom God always intended you to be.

Prayer is a relationship. Living in a Navy community, we are privy to some of life's most dramatic moments. In the community it is common for groups to gather hours before a ship's expected arrival time, looking out beyond the horizon for a fleck of gray to pop up with the rising sun. It has been six months, six long, lonely, heartbreaking months that their loved ones have been away at war. Births, deaths, joy, and sorrow can happen many times in half a year. Lovers ache for an embrace; children long to be tossed on a knee. Mothers just want to see the face they have missed for so long. The gangplank scrapes to a stop and sailors salute, break rank, and race to outstretched arms.

"As a deer longs for flowing streams, so my soul longs for you, O God" (Ps. 42:1).

Some of us have been away from God a long time. Our hearts long for God, but it is as if God is out to sea, and we await God's return. Your wait is over. God is coming today. God is running to you like a father greeting a long-lost son. God's arms are wide apart. Open your arms to God!

Prayer is a relationship with God. How is your relationship with the Lord? If prayer is a relationship, then what is important is not what you know, but whom you know. In prayer, our relationship with Jesus makes all the difference. He said, "Whenever you ask my father in my name, God will honor your request" (John 16:23, paraphr.).

Do you know Jesus Christ well enough to use his name when you talk with his Father? That kind of relationship makes all the difference.

41

Prayer, Part 2

Philippians 1:3-11;
Psalm 51:3-10, 92:1

A Midwestern farming community struggled through two seasons of drought. In a last-ditch effort to break the dry spell, they asked the local clergy to hold a prayer meeting and pray for rain. The church was packed. One pastor after another prayed for the skies to open up and rain down on the parched earth. The last pastor to pray was the Presbyterian minister. She took the pulpit and said, "You have all come here this evening to pray for rain."

"Amen", the overflowing congregation shouted.

"Well, do you think you have sufficient faith?"

"Amen," they shouted.

"Okay, I believe you. But one thing is troubling me." The crowd grew quiet and tense, waiting for the minister to explain.

"One thing is troubling me. Where are your umbrellas?"

Do you believe faithful prayers are answered? Then don't forget your umbrella!

Our contemporary Presbyterian catechism, *Belonging to God,* teaches us *how* to pray.

Q. 47. What do we do when we pray?

A. 47. When we pray, we adore God, we confess our sins, we give God thanks, and we pray for the needs of others and ourselves.

There is an easy way to remember what goes into a prayer. The acronym ACTS, as in the book of the Acts of the Apostles, spells out the contents of a good prayer. A: Adoration; C: Confession; T: Thanksgiving; S: Supplication.

The catechism uses this formula as an outline for effective prayer.

A: Adoration

Back in 1984, when our denomination was researching for an updated *Book of Common Worship,* a preliminary book on contemporary worship was published (*The Service for the Lord's Day*) that explained the workings of worship as the church. The instructions for worship say that the first thing we need to do is give God praise. That's adoration. "God is good—all the time! All the time—God is good!" That's adoration! This helpful book on worship says: "Adoration is the keynote of all true worship, of the creature before the Creator, of the redeemed before the Redeemer. In song and prayer, God is praised."[47]

When you pray, begin with praise: "Praise God, from whom all blessings flow!"

C: Confession

The prophet Nathan reported to King David that a wealthy man, who had flocks of sheep but did not want to give up any, went to a poor neighbor who had only one lamb, a lamb that was like a pet, and took it to feed his company. King David was furious and told Nathan that the man who did this must pay four times the usual penalty.

Nathan answered, "It is you!"

David had stolen a man's wife and then had ordered him killed. His sin lay bare before God. King David confessed, saying: "Be merciful to me, O God, because of your constant love. Because of your great mercy wipe away my sins! Wash away all my evil and make me clean from my sin! I recognize my faults; I am always conscious of my sins. I have sinned against you—only against you—and done what you consider evil. . . . Create a pure heart in me, O God, and put a new and loyal spirit in me" (Ps. 51:1–4a, 10 TEV).

We confess our sins.

T: Thanksgiving

A cartoon in the Sunday paper shows a little boy looking disappointed at the leftovers being served for supper. He says, "We asked God to bless this LAST night." At mealtime, we give thanks, even for leftovers! In all things give thanks to God, the Bible says. An old gospel song tells us to count our blessings one by one. "Thanks a lot!" should be a prayer we pray every day. At the table, our main prayer in the service of Communion is called the Eucharistic Prayer. That term *eucharistic* comes from a Greek word meaning thanksgiving. You will notice that the prayer is basically saying, "Thanks **a lot,** Lord!"

In prayer we give thanks to God.

S: Supplication

Supplication means asking God to act in our lives and in the lives of others. In a children's sermon, a pastor asked the children if they prayed every day. One boy answered, "No, not every day. Sometimes I don't want anything." Sadly, some adults still think of prayer this way. Supplication is lifting your heartfelt concerns to God and trusting that God will hear, respond, and act in a way that best fits God's plan for us.

Last fall I attended a workshop with Dr. Brian Wren, professor of worship at Columbia Seminary. He is a theologian and also a hymn writer. He reminded us that when we pray in church we do not have to keep saying, ". . . if it be your will, Lord." I am sure you have heard prayers like that. He said that we do not have to keep reminding God to check the divine game plan for us. God knows it by heart. Just pray: Lord, heal her; Lord, give him peace; Lord, help me through today; Lord, let justice be done; Lord, forgive me; Lord, change me; Lord, let me forgive; Lord, hold me close to you. Just pray what's on your mind; God will do the rest.

ACTS: Adoration-Confession-Thanksgiving-Supplication

When we pray, we adore God, we confess our sins, we give God thanks, and we pray for the needs of others and ourselves. Simple. Straightforward. Real. Effective.

42

The Jesus Prayer 1

Matthew 6:5-8

Where do you get answers to life's big questions?

Charlie Brown's little sister goes to her big brother. Charlie Brown is comfortably watching television from an overstuffed easy chair. His sister comes in with paper in hand. "I have to write a report for school on the secret of life. Can you give me some suggestions?" Charlie Brown, without looking away from the TV, says, "Turn off appliances when not in use, form car pools, and defrost foods before cooking." She walks away, disappointed, saying, "I'll go ask someone else."

Where do you go to get life's big questions answered? The apostles went to Jesus. In Luke's Gospel, the Twelve asked Jesus one of those big questions, "Will you teach us to pray, just as John the Baptist taught his disciples a new way to pray?" (Luke 11:1, paraphr.). When Jesus said, "Pray like this," he was carrying on the rabbinical tradition of teaching by providing his disciples with a better way to improve on the prayer practices of the religious elite (Matt. 6:5–8).

Our contemporary catechism follows this long tradition of teaching disciples how to pray. In the preceding chapter we learned that an effective contemporary prayer has four components—adoration and praise (A), confession of sin (C), thanksgiving (T), and supplication (S). Now we learn how Jesus himself answered the big question, "How should we pray?"

Q. 48. How did Jesus teach his followers to pray?
A. 48. He taught them the words of the Lord's Prayer.

"Our Father, who art in heaven, hallowed be your name . . . ." You know the rest. Why did Jesus direct us to pray to the God of heaven and earth, the God of Abraham, Sarah, Moses, Miriam, and David?

Jesus did so because God is the Author of life.

Narratives that we read or see performed sometimes are lovely and have satisfying endings. Other times, they take us on journeys tangential to the story line, and their endings leave us scratching our heads. The storyteller controls the narrative. Life is like a tale that is told. Some lives are rich and full. My aunt May is heading into her final days. Born in 1906, she has seen the world change before her eyes. She was trapped in Belgium at the outbreak of World War I while visiting relatives there. She gave birth to her babies at home, as was the custom then. She prospered as a housewife and mother during the Depression years and sent her son off to the Navy in the 1950s. She raised me as an infant while my mother was recuperating from tuberculosis. She managed while her husband was laid off from the factory. She traveled across the country and sailed on the oceans. She learned to drive as a senior citizen and watched men walk on the moon in the summer of 1969. She traveled until early this year. Her life has been rich and faith-filled. What a story!

Other lives are too brief. My nephew Christopher's life was much too short. Complications in an emergency room cut his story short and we still grieve for a boy who saw only a few years of life. It is the right of authors to tell their stories. An author may have the story linger on long after the point is made, or challenge us by ending it too soon. Still, it is the author's tale to tell. God is the Author of creation, of all that is. God allows us to develop and grow and tell our story as human beings, but ultimately God is in charge of the plot and the number of pages. Our prayer must be addressed to the One who writes the script.

The One who writes the script is the One who is Love.

There is a story about a farmer who had a weather vane on his barn. The iron arrow had a motto painted on it that read, *God is love.* The farmer was asked if the motto intended to suggest that God's love is as changeable as the weather. "Oh, no!" the farmer said. "It means that no matter which way the winds blow, God is love." For many, this is the secret of life, the secret of being content and having a quiet heart. To know that God's love is constant and is in action no matter which way the winds are blowing in your life is a great blessing. This is why Jesus directed us to pray to the God of heaven and earth and all that is, was, and ever will be.

Prayer is a relationship that we have with the Author of life and love.

To say that prayer is a relationship tells us that we have a part to play. Freedom makes relationships possible. We are free to let go and let God. We are free to walk hand in hand with Jesus and even let him carry us when we can no longer walk by our own strength. We are free to break away from our self-centeredness and latch on to God's will and plan for our lives. We are also free to ignore God. We are free to do what *we* want, not what God wants. We are free to make poor choices, to think of ourselves before others and all else, to store up treasure on earth instead of in heaven, to walk right on by those who are hurt or who need help, or even to discount God's plan for us and the ways in which God so masterfully places us in just the right spot with just the right purpose.

We are free to work out our own way in life, and maybe in the end we will come to the place where God wants us to be. Often, on our own, we end up taking the long way around. But if we had sought God's guidance, we could have had a much easier way of it. We pray to the God of heaven and earth because God has a plan for us that is much better than anything we can produce on our own.

Why pray to the God of heaven and earth? Because Jesus tells us to, that's why. Who better to listen to when it comes to the big questions in life than the one who knows God's mind and heart? When the one who knows God says to pray in a certain way, are you going to argue? So pray this way: "Our Father in heaven . . . ."

Jesus' particular phrasing may have been new at the time, but prayer was not new. God has been communicating with humanity since God took long walks in the garden with Adam and Eve. Talking bushes and donkeys, mountaintop experiences, and a gentle and still small voice have all been different modes of God's interaction with God's people. God spoke through the prophets and then most clearly in Jesus of Nazareth. And the message has been much the same thing: "You are my beloved."

> Yes, I have loved you with an everlasting love.
> I have always loved you—
> I have loved you through all your experiences.
> I have loved you in the times when you wandered far
>   from me.
> I have loved you when you doubted.
> I have loved you when you did not see the way.
> I have loved you when you thought that I did not hear you.
> I have loved you in your triumphs.
> I have loved you in your times of despair.
> I have loved you in your times of joy and
> I have loved you when your heart needed comfort.
> I love you with an everlasting love that never falters,
>   never fails.
> I love you always and eternally.
> I love you with an enduring love that takes no account
>   of mistakes but sees only the growth you are making—the
>   steps you are taking from darkness into light;
> the measure of faith you are achieving.
> Yes, I love you with an everlasting love. (Jer. 31:3, paraphr.)
>   Your heavenly Father

43
The Jesus Prayer 2
Romans 8:15-16

According to an article in the *Virginian Pilot*, Rick Husband, the commander of the space shuttle *Columbia*, looked out the window of his spacecraft and saw what he called God's awe-inspiring creation. Crew member Michael Anderson, a physicist, said he believed heaven, not space, was the final frontier. Their faith may come as a surprise to those who think that science and religion are on irreconcilable paths. The space program has a long history of astronauts who have boldly taken their faith into orbit, beginning with John Glenn in 1958. Glenn became the first American to orbit the earth, and in 1998, at age seventy-seven, he returned to space on the shuttle *Discovery*. He noted that it is impossible to look out the window of the shuttle and not to believe in God.

Religion was a palpable presence on board the *Columbia* in its final mission. On board was a palm-size Torah carried by Ilan Ramon of Israel. And on January 17, 2003, at 11:39 A.M. the *Columbia* crew bowed their heads in reverent silence to honor the exact moment the space shuttle *Challenger* had exploded in the skies seventeen years earlier almost to the day. Many scientists say their faith buttresses their studies. In this age in which space exploration is no longer the novelty it was forty years ago, when we think of the Lord's Prayer and its beginning words, "Our Father who art in heaven," it is natural for our thoughts to break the bonds of earth's gravity and launch our thoughts beyond, where no one has ever gone before. The beginning words of the Lord's Prayer take us on a linguistic roller-coaster ride, high and low, and low and high, with a G-force equal to that of a rocket launch.

The God of the Universe, the Cosmic God, Lord of Heaven, Creator God, Totally Other, Primordial Being, First Cause, Prime Source, Alpha/Omega, God of gods, Lord of lords, Mighty God, Everlasting Father, Transcendent and Omnipotent Maker of heaven and earth, Great I AM. Our Father who art in heaven, holy is your name!

In this same beginning phrase, however, the words strain like brakes and push us in a whole new direction, as we hear ourselves say of this same God: Papa! Daddy! *Abba ho Pater!* Our Father. The beginning words juxtapose the grandest language we can muster with the most intimate—the transcendent with the personal. One phrase says in the same breath that God is cosmic and God is intimate. Our contemporary catechism, *Belonging to God*, explains these beginning words:

Q. 50. What do we mean when we pray to God as "Our Father"?

A. 50. As Jesus taught us, we call upon God like little children who know that God cares for them and loves them. Because Jesus prayed to God as his Father, we too can pray to God in this way.

The apostle Paul wrote: "Because you are children, God has sent the Spirit of his Son into our hearts, crying, 'Abba! Father!' (Gal. 4:6). When Jesus said to pray to God as our Father, he was introducing a fresh and innovative way to pray. The terminology "Our Father" is not found in the Old Testament. The Jewish rabbis were reluctant to apply this informal title to Yahweh, the God of Abraham and Moses. It was not until the end of the first century A.D. that rabbis started to use the term "Our Father" in their prayers, and then only infrequently.

Contrast this with scores of times the title "Father" is used in the New Testament. It is found in the Gospels over 125 times, and not one of these instances is part of prayer. When this title is used, however, it carries the meaning found in the Lord's Prayer: Abba, Father—*Abba ho Pater* in Greek—Dearest Father.

Until recently, it was thought that *Abba* was a word that developed from Aramaic, the language Jesus spoke. The Palestinian Aramaic word for "father" is *ab*. It has generally been believed that the informal reference to "my father" or "daddy" developed from the formal word for "father." Recent studies are suggesting that it may be much simpler. Just as "dada" or "mama," basic sounds that babies are able to make, have come to mean father or mother, the primitive sound "ab-ba" may be the source of the biblical word *ab*, father. If so, it highlights the evocation of intense personal and primal emotions when used in prayer to God. The God who effortlessly spun the galaxies into being like cotton candy on a paper stick is the God our most human instinct calls "loving parent."

> In first century Rome, an emperor celebrated a victorious military campaign by leading his legions through the streets of Rome. Along the route, a platform had been erected where the empress and the emperor's family could sit and observe the procession. As that procession approached the platform, the emperor's little son jumped down from the platform . . . and started to run out to the road to meet his father's chariot. A Roman soldier . . . spotted the boy, held him back, and said, "You can't run out there! Don't you know that's the emperor?" The boy laughed and replied: "He may be your emperor, but he's my father!"[48]

When Jesus prayed, he called God "Abba, Father." Only one possible English translation of this Aramaic word fits, and that is "daddy."

Scholars tell us that no Jew in Jesus' day would dare use the word "Abba" for God. Jesus, on the other hand, encouraged the church to pray this way. For us, when we pray using the words "Our Father or Father God," or "Divine Loving Parent," we are blending the awesomeness of the Cosmic God with the intensity of Emmanuel, God with us.

When we pray, "Our Father . . ." we are expressing both an ultimate reverence for and an intensely personal reliance on God. The beginning words of the Lord's Prayer announce God's *totally other* nature while also drawing on the most primal of human needs—totally trusting a loving parent to care for and love us. In just two words, "Our Father," we say so much. We place God in a right theology, we see ourselves realistically, and we set the stage for effective prayer.

44

The Jesus Prayer 3

John 4:24; Genesis 1:27; Isaiah 66:13; Matthew 23:37

A family vacationed in Colorado. The Rocky Mountains rose majestically in the distance. The motel room's window opened up to the grandeur of the snow-capped display of nature. The mother, father, and their son stood looking out the window in awe. The parents began to muse about how God, long ago, with the heart of an artist, crafted the wonders that stood before them. The little boy asked, "Well, what's He been doing lately?"

Don Carruthers served as stated supply pastor of Petersburg-Bethel Presbyterian Church in Central Pennsylvania prior to my ministry there. One of his stories recalled a night many years ago when he was still a student at Princeton Seminary. A seasoned professor, who knew forty or more Semitic languages, visited his room. The professor's son, an archaeologist, had died in the Middle East. His daughter was critically ill at the time. Rev. Carruthers remembered the professor confiding in him his deep, personal convictions. The professor said, "Carruthers, the greatest mystery is why God should reveal Himself at all!"

What do these two stories have in common? Both speak of the mystery of God. Both refer to the wonder and awe of God. And both call God "He." Our contemporary catechism helps us deal with the way we traditionally address God as masculine.

Q. 51. When we pray to God as our Father, do we mean that God is male?

Many would say yes. And without thinking deeply, you may think so too, especially when Jesus himself called God his Father and tells us to pray like this: "Our Father in heaven." It is true, Jesus does say to pray like this, but is he saying that God is male?

Some would say that we refer to God as a male because the Old and New Testaments were written at times when the male was the more powerful gender in society. This is quite true. Our Bible emerged from a patriarchal culture. Some, finding offense in this, choose to avoid any gender-specific language at all when talking about God. For many of them the Trinity is not

God the Father, Son, and Holy Spirit but rather God—Creator, Redeemer, and Sanctifier. They avoid any reference to God as male.

Others have chosen to flip convention on its head. In Andrew Greeley's Father Blackie mysteries, the auxiliary bishop always refers to God as "She." It is startling until you get used to it. Yet others have chosen to try to avoid controversy by including all gender references in one shot, to cover all the bases by praying "Mother/Father/Parent God."

Some have tried to avoid controversy by stripping God of any personality. During the Reign of Terror, the National Assembly declared France a nation of atheists. This brief experience convinced them that living without God would destroy the nation. Robespierre proclaimed that belief in the existence of God was necessary if a nation were to have law and order, and the national representatives passed a measure into law that acknowledged the existence of the Supreme Being. However, this statement was based on a generic belief in a god no one could come to know in a personal way.

For the Old Testament church, calling God by a gender-specific name was not an issue. For the Israelites, just saying God's name was considered an affront to the Creator. Devout Jews, had they spoken English, would not have spelled out God but would have expressed the word by writing G_D. They knew and addressed God as YHWH,[50] which we pronounce "Yahweh." When copying the Scriptures onto a new scroll, the scribe took out a new quill pen with new ink to write the name Yahweh. Before writing it, he was required to say, "I intend to write the Name of God." If the scribe failed to do this, the whole scroll was ruined. God's name continues to be held in such esteem that devout Jews today do not call God personal names like "our Father." For devout Jews, gender-specific language is not an issue. However, for many contemporary Christians it is.

Q. 51. When we pray to God as our Father, do we mean that God is male?

A. 51. No. Only creatures who have bodies can be male or female. But God is Spirit and has no body.

It was not that long ago that we still used all-male references when we talked or wrote about God. It was not long ago that we were a male-oriented society. It was easy to relate God to males and acceptable to equate God with maleness. A story goes that football coach Vince Lombardi climbed into bed on a cold Green Bay night and his wife, Marie, said, "God, your feet are ice cold!" The famous coach answered, "Dear, in the privacy of our own home, you may call me Vince."

It was not that long ago that the word "humankind" started to replace "mankind" in presidential speeches. "Chairperson" became the norm instead of "chairman." You may remember that just a decade or two ago we were told it was proper to write "he or she" anytime we wanted to refer to a nonspecific person. The new Presbyterian hymnal is gender neutral as we sing, "Good Christians Friends, Rejoice" instead of the traditional "Good Christian Men, Rejoice."

Inclusive language has become very important to us in the church in our prayers, hymns, and writings. We have come to understand that some words can exclude whole groups of people in certain contexts. I tend to call a group "guys" no matter who is there, and when I do I am sure that some feel excluded. So, when we pray "Our Father . . ." are we saying that God is male?

No. Biblical theology tells us that only those with a physical body can have gender: ". . . male and female God created them." (Gen. 1:27b, paraphr.). People have bodies and we are male and female. God is Spirit and God is not male or female—or both. God is Spirit. When thinking about God and how to describe God, John Calvin once said that God's nature is immeasurable and spiritual. "The Scriptural teaching concerning God's infinite and spiritual essence ought to be enough, not only to banish popular delusions but also to refute the subtleties of secular philosophy"[50] In other words, he is saying, "When something defies description, let it."

Talking about our Creator God, John Gibson says, "Human words like human thought belong this side of Creation and cannot begin to describe its other side, God as he is in his own interior life." In himself, God is "before" time and "beyond" space, and only enters time and space because he wants to. In himself, God is Wholly Other.[51]

Gibson uses male language to reference God, even in an explanation that God is indescribable. Why? Because Jesus gave Christians permission to address the Lord of the Cosmos in a personal and intimate way as Father by creating a relationship between God and us as personal and intimate as a child reaching out to a loving parent.

Theologian John Macquarrie writes,

God is represented in the Bible as incomparable: "To whom then will you liken God?" [Isa. 40:18]. . . . But the more usual theological expression is "incomprehensible." So in the Athanasian Creed: "The Father incomprehensible, the Son incomprehensible and the Holy Ghost incomprehensible." God . . . is suprarational, and escapes the grasp of our intellect. But on the other hand, the adjectives "incomparable," "incomprehensible," "suprarational," do not imply that God . . . is just a cipher, an empty name. . . . As both transcendent and immanent, God is at once beyond every possible being, yet present in every one of these beings. God points us to the paradox; God is both hidden and manifest.[52]

Calling God "he" or "she" is just our human way of making our relationship with God personal. Jesus opened the way for this more intimate relationship with the Creator God. He said, "Pray this way . . ." and advised us to relate to God as a loving parent, as *Our Father*. Thank you, Jesus, for gifting us with an Emmanuel experience with God!

I trust you realize that no matter how we address God—he, she, Lord, or Spirit—we can never fully box God into our human concepts and categories. In fact, the more we think about it, the more we will realize that God is just too wonderful and amazing for our minds to fully comprehend. The names and titles and pronouns we use in our prayers do not impact God's very nature or the fact that God loves us with a love that will not let go. I think this is what the great medieval theologian Thomas Aquinas must have come to find out. He created one of the greatest intellectual achievements of Western civilization in his *Summa theologica*, a massive work of thirty-eight treatises, three thousand articles, and ten thousand objections. Thomas tried to gather all of truth into one coherent whole. What an undertaking—anthropology, science, ethics, psychology, political theory, and theology, all under God!

One day, Thomas abruptly stopped writing. In worship, he had sensed a glimpse of eternity and suddenly knew that all his work of describing God fell far short of God's reality. He decided never to write again. Even the greatest minds realize they cannot fathom the greatness of God. God is beyond human descriptions because God is divine and thus totally Other.

Amen.

45

The Jesus Prayer 4

Psalm 14:2; 1 Kings 22:19;
2 Kings 19:5

As we explore the text of the Lord's Prayer, our contemporary catechism breaks down the phrases of the prayer and highlights each important truth.

Q. 52. What do we mean when we pray to God "in heaven"?

A. 52. We mean that God draws near to us from beyond this world and hears our prayers.

In Jesus' day, when someone talked about a god drawing near to people from beyond this world, most would automatically have thought of Prometheus. It was not a good thing for divinity to draw near to human beings from the other side of heaven!

Prometheus was a Greek god. In the days before human beings domesticated fire, life was harsh and painful. In pity, Prometheus took fire from heaven and gave it as a gift to humanity. Zeus, the king of the gods, was angry that earthly beings should enjoy the use of fire. So he took Prometheus and chained him to a rock in the middle of the Adriatic Sea, where the heat of the sun and the cold of the night tortured him unceasingly. Further, Zeus sent a vulture to tear out Prometheus' liver, which daily reappeared only to be torn out again and again and again. This was a typical reprisal from the other side of heaven. In the ancient world, it appears that people thought the gods were jealous and vengeful and grudging. The last thing the gods wanted was to find a way to enter human life from their heavenly perch and help humankind.

Yet when Jesus prayed, "Our Father, who art in heaven," he was revealing that God actually does come to us from beyond this world and becomes personal in our lives. But locating God as a "heavenly God' functions as a cautionary discipline for the church. It is a continuing reminder that our God is holy and powerful, a heavenly Lord, not just a god who fits neatly into a shirt pocket or rides the dashboard like a plastic statue. We are cautioned not to think of God as an earthly parent, limited as we are. God is our heavenly Father.

Like many of you, I am a parent. I love my sons and would give my life for their safety and would sacrifice my livelihood for their well-being. Yet there are limits to what my love can do for them. I may love my sons very much but I may not be able to help them achieve something or stop them from doing something harmful. My love can be intense yet helpless. My fatherly love can be strong, yet just because I love them I cannot keep bad things from happening to them. I cannot guarantee they will not fail or make mistakes or even turn away from me, a father who loves them very, very much. All parents know this. Anyone who has ever loved someone knows that love is limited in its power.

Suffering from a cold recently, I went home early a few days and just "vegged out." One day I watched Dr. Phil on television. His show was about parents who loved their children, but wanted them to get out on their own. Having grown children living at home, taking advantage of Mom and Dad's love and parental concern, was starting to drive them crazy. One couple wanted Dr. Phil to tell their two adult sons (twenty- and thirty-year-olds) to "get out and start taking care of themselves."

Dr. Phil, in his slow North Carolina drawl, asked, "Do you want me to tell them for you to 'get out'?"

"Yes" the parents said, telling him they loved their sons but could not seem to get the message across.

"OK," Dr. Phil said. "GET OUT!" Everyone laughed. It is what the parents should have done long ago, but their love kept them from being strong. Our earthly, parental love is limited in its power. We try to help our children, but often our earthly love is not strong enough to have us do what is needed at the moment. Every parent knows this. Anyone who has ever loved someone knows that love is limited in its power.

But when we say, "Our Father . . . in heaven," we speak a spiritual truth that claims that God's love is powerful beyond the love of this world. Bible scholar William Barclay writes: "When we say 'Our Father—in heaven' . . . we tell ourselves that the power of God is always motivated by the love of God, and can never be exercised for anything but our good; we tell ourselves that the love of God is always backed by the power of God, and that therefore its purposes can never be ultimately frustrated or defeated."[53] God's love is powerful and without limits; human love, like that shown by parents, is powerful, yet limited. When we pray, "Our Father . . . in heaven," we are cautioned not to think of God's love for us in earthly terms.

I remember someone trying to worm her way out of a sticky situation in which she was the guilty party. She caused a lot of pain in a church conflict. She did not realize how much hurt she inflicted on other church members. She flippantly stated that everyone should just forgive her because, after all, God forgave her—that is God's job! This is a person who confused earthly love with heavenly love. It is like confusing God with David Huxley.

Back in 1997 David Huxley strapped a harness around his waist. The other end of the harness was hooked to a 187-ton Boeing 747 airliner. With his tennis shoes firmly planted on the runway, Huxley leaned forward and pulled with all his might. Remarkably, he was able to get the jetliner rolling down the runway. In fact he pulled the 747 one hundred yards in eighty seconds. Let's say human love is David Huxley. It can do amazing things. But God's love is like a jet pilot who takes her seat behind the controls of the 747 and fires up the engines and takes the jetliner five miles high and flies ten thousand miles across the world.

When we pray, "Our Father . . . in heaven," we speak a spiritual truth that claims that God's love is powerful beyond the love of this world. Love unlimited! Love undefeated! Love only a heavenly God can give. Have you opened your life to God's love? If not, why not do so today?

46
The Jesus Prayer 5
Leviticus 20:26; Numbers 15:40; Deuteronomy 5:11

God's name is holy! We are not to disrespect it.

Our contemporary catechism asks:

Q. 53. What do we ask when we pray "Hallowed be your name"?

A. 53. We pray that God's name will be honored in all the world and everywhere treated as holy, because God's name really stands for God.

When Jesus instructs us to include "Hallowed be your name," he harks back to the divine commandment not to use God's name in less than honorable fashion.

When Moses approached the burning bush he must have peeled off his baseball cap and scratched his head wondering why it was on fire but not burning up. When a heavenly voice came from the bush a moment later, he had no more need to wonder—it was the voice of God! "Call me Yahweh," God said, "because I am who I am." That name, the name God told us to use, is to be honored and never defiled, according to the Third Commandment. The Jews of Jesus' day did not speak that name or write out the word God when they meant Yahweh, the Lord of life, and some Jews today will not. In the Jesus Prayer, the phrase "hallowed be your name" is a rephrasing of the Third Commandment: "You shall not take the Lord's name in vain."

William Barclay translated Jesus' words thus: "Let your name be held holy."[54] In trying to understand why Jesus included the words "hallowed be thy name" in the Lord's Prayer, Clarence Jordan, author of *The Cotton Patch Gospels*, writes that Jesus was all too aware of the human tendency toward hypocrisy. To call God "Father" implies that the speakers claim to be God's children without regard to the way they behave. Through this kind of false intimacy, human beings take God's name in vain. In this way, God's children use the Father's holy name to hide their shameful sinfulness. "Jesus wanted no such people among his followers. Citizens of his kingdom—'*Christ-ians*'—

were given a new name, and he intended that they should take it seriously and sincerely, and keep it ever sacred and holy." Only the sincere are able to pray that God's name be hallowed.[55]

It is only those who hallow God's name who will find meaning in the rest of the Lord's Prayer. In Greek, the word "hallow" comes from a word we translate as "holy." But it means more than just "spiritual." It is a word used to describe a person or thing that is treated in a spiritually reverential way. An institution that is hallowed means a place or religious item set apart for worship and devotion. Our children love to play in our beautiful new church building, running and making their voices echo in the brick atrium. But when they come into the sanctuary, I ask them to treat this space with respect because it is where we worship the Lord. No running or jumping on the stairs is allowed. This is the holy space where we meet God in worship.

The Lord's Day is holy, and different from the other six, or at least it ought to be for us. When we use the term "holy" in heavenly ways, we are led to the place where we can say, "Let God's name be treated differently from all other names—let God's name be given a position which is absolutely unique."[56]

Add to the Greek meaning of the word "hallowed" the Hebrew understanding of one's name, and this phrase takes us even deeper into the mind of Jesus when he said, "Pray this way . . . ." In Old Testament culture, one's name was not only what your mother yelled when it was time for supper; it was also an indicator of your character and personality. For example, the name Jacob means "heel grabber," and Jacob lived that out as he grabbed for his older brother's blessing and birthright. "Moses" means "drawn out." Moses was indeed saved from the Nile River as a baby, and he also drew the Hebrews out from Egypt. Obed was the grandfather of King David, and the name Obed means worshiper. The prophet Elijah's name means "my God is Yahweh." "Elisha," the name of his protégé, means "God saves." Hagar was Sarah's servant and the mother of Ishmael. Her name means "flight," and she was forced to take flight on her own with her son into the Arabian Desert. Old Testament names portray the character and personality of persons.

This is also true for the names of God. In English, we say "Lord" or "God," but in Hebrew there are a variety of names for God: *Yahweh, El Shaddai, El Elyon, El Olam, El Roi, El Bethel, Elohim, Adonai.*

Theologian Emil Brunner wrote: "God Himself is known where His name is made known. . . . The gift of knowledge of His name is an act of grace. . . . Those who know God's grace, through knowing His name, are thereby led into a relationship of trust and confidence in Him."[57] God's name displays God's character and intentions. When we put together "hallowed" and the name of God, we are saying along with Jesus, "Let us give you, Yahweh, the highest praise and exalted place in our lives that your divine nature and character deserve." My friend Ed was someone whose love of God was transparent. Although he was a man of great intellect, accomplishments, and adventures, his life was such that it revealed that his highest praise and most sincere respect were for God.

I stopped by a restaurant on Friday for lunch. It was crowded and noisy. Three men on lunch break were in the booth next to mine. Two immediately started eating when the food came. The third bowed his head and whispered a prayer. He radiated peace, even though he was in a military uniform. He may work for a commander at the NATO base and pledge his loyalty to a commander-in-chief in the White House, but his highest respect and admiration clearly was for his God.

The president recently held a press conference, and he was asked an unusual question. A man wondered how his faith was sustaining him at this pressure-packed time. He answered that he prays for guidance and wisdom daily and that the countless anonymous prayers by citizens that lift him and his family up to the throne of grace bolster him greatly. He acknowledged that he will never know these people but said it was their prayers that sustained him. Here is the man who most say is the most powerful person on earth, honoring God by reverently accepting the prayers offered on his behalf to the God whose name is held in ultimate respect, even by the most powerful man on earth.

When you pray, "Hallowed be thy name," you too are holding God's name in ultimate reverence, indicating that you know God by name.

Yahweh: Ever-present/ever-existent God.
El Shaddai: All-powerful God.
El Elyon: Most High God.
El Olam: the Everlasting God.
El Roi: God who sees me.
El Bethel: Elohim . . . Adonai.
Amen.

47
The Jesus Prayer 6
Mark 14:25, 36; Psalm 103:19

O ur investigation of the Lord's Prayer takes us to the next question from our contemporary catechism, *Belonging to God*.

Q. 54. What do we ask when we pray, "Your kingdom come, your will be done, on earth as in heaven"?

A. 54. We ask God to fulfill God's purpose for the whole world. We also ask God to make us able and willing to accept God's will in all things, and to do our part in bringing about God's purpose.

In funeral services I often reflect on our strong belief that God has a plan for us in life. One of the best-known Scripture texts that describes God's plan for us is a poetic segment of Ecclesiastes, an Old Testament book of wisdom. The word "Ecclesiastes" means "the preacher," and this unnamed preacher reminds us that God is more interested in the things on our hearts, however rough, than in the polished words we use to impress God. So in simple words and a few easy-to-remember phrases, the Preacher explains:

> There is a time for everything, and a season for every activity
>   under heaven:
> a time to be born and a time to die,
> a time to plant and a time to uproot,
> a time to kill and a time to heal,
> a time to tear down and a time to build,
> a time to weep and a time to laugh, . . .
> a time to tear and a time to mend,
> a time to be silent and a time to speak,
> a time to love and a time to hate,
> a time for war and a time for peace.[58]

In God's time, life will unfold and we will exist, the world will turn and God's purpose will come to pass.

About 350 years later, another Jewish preacher said, "Pray this way: thy kingdom come, thy will be done, on earth as it is in heaven." In a way, he was saying something similar—pray that God's will and purpose will come to pass in our present-day situation as well as in eternity. Our contemporary catechism breaks this down into three very applicable prayer requests. These are prayers we can pray and really mean what we pray.

A. 54(a). We ask God to fulfill God's purpose for the whole world.

Psalm 103:19 says that God's kingdom is already functioning whenever God's purposes are acted out. "The LORD has established his throne in the heavens, and his kingdom rules over all." In other words, God's got the whole world in his hands. God is working out the divine purpose in the present tense. Yet the kingdom of God will be fully known and will become the operational pattern for living at some time in the future. Jesus said at the Last Supper, "I will never again drink of the fruit of the vine until that day when I drink it new in the kingdom of God" (Mark 14:25). It seems to me that Jesus was saying that we live in a both/and world—God's kingdom is now and God's kingdom is in the future. Maybe that is not a difficult reality for God to grasp, but it is nearly impossible for human beings to understand. God's kingdom has come, yet we are so far from living it out.

The people of the Florida panhandle recently felt just how far away we are from the kingdom of God. In what seemed to have been to be a political move to scare the living daylights out of the leaders of "rogue nations," we dropped MOAB, the mother of all bombs. It shook the earth for dozens of miles and sent a mushroom cloud ten miles into the air. MOAB, the Massive Ordnance Air Blast, is the largest conventional weapon in our arsenal. Its power is just short of a nuclear bomb. I am not sure if the name MOAB was chosen intentionally because it is a biblical name. However, Moab was indeed the name of Lot's son, and it means "of the father." To me, it just brings home the reality of how far we are from God's will being done on earth. We are so far from the kingdom at times. So Jesus says to pray that our world will be more and more like God's heavenly kingdom. And someday, I trust, God's will and purpose will be acted out on earth just as it is in heaven, and it will once again be a time for peace.

Hanging in the Worcester Art Museum in Massachusetts is the American artist Edward Hicks's famous painting, *The Peaceable Kingdom*. Painted in 1833, it depicts Isaiah's vision of a world of peace where "the wolf shall live with the lamb, the leopard shall lie down with the kid, the calf and the lion and the fatling together, and a little child shall lead them" (Isa. 11:6–7). Huddled together are natural enemies, predator and prey, living in perfect harmony. A little child sits among them, safe and happy. Hicks painted over one hundred copies of *The Peaceable Kingdom,* and in many of these he included a scene of William Penn signing a peace treaty with the Indians. Hicks believed that the future kingdom of God is partially experienced on earth in our day when people find ways to live together in peace. We pray that God's kingdom can be experienced here while it reflects that which is a constant there, in heaven.

A. 54(b). We also ask God to make us able and willing to accept God's will in all things.

Jesus prayed, "Remove this cup from me; yet, not what I want, but what you want" (Mark 14:36).

Thomas "Stonewall" Jackson, professor at Virginia Military Institute, Presbyterian elder, and general in the Civil War, is the main character in the movie *Gods and Generals*. As a devout man of God, Jackson put his total trust in God as he went into battle, even when he struggled for his own life after being wounded by friendly fire. At one point, he told his wife to pray for him, but he followed up by encouraging her to always pray that God's will be done. He was so determined to do God's will that every action, decision, and prayer was buttressed with "your will be done." In the end, he accepted God's will for his life, and in the shade of the trees he saw himself on "the other side," in the kingdom of God.

Paul wrote: "For the kingdom of God is not food and drink but righteousness and peace and joy in the Holy Spirit" (Rom. 14:17). There seems to be a special peace for those who can say with Stonewall Jackson, "Thy will be done." However, Christianity isn't a passive acquiescence to some invisible and deterministic force. Our catechism adds:

A. 54(c). We ask God to make us able and willing to do our part in bringing about God's purpose.

More than one hundred years ago, D. L. Moody said: "Pray as if everything depends on God, and work as if everything depends on you." Good advice then, and good advice now for contemporary Christians! When you pray, pray this way: "Your kingdom come, Lord, and your will and purpose be done here on earth, reflecting your heavenly desire for your people." Amen.

48
The Jesus Prayer 7
Exodus 16:4; Luke 12:22-24; James 1:17

G ive us this day our daily bread" seems like it should be the easiest and most direct of the phrases of the Lord's Prayer to understand. It may surprise you, however, that there are a variety of ways the church has understood this over the centuries. Our contemporary catechism, *Belonging to God*, asks:

Q. 55. Why do we pray "Give us today our daily bread"?

A. 55. Because all good things come from God. Even in our most ordinary needs, God cares for us completely.

This is simple, straightforward, and easy to understand for contemporary Christians, yes? In past days it was not so easy.

At one time, "daily bread" was understood to mean the bread of the Lord's Table. From the earliest days of the church, the Lord's Prayer has always been connected with the Lord's Supper. Even today, we say the Jesus Prayer as part of our celebration of Communion. The bread was understood to mean that each day, we were to receive the Communion bread and be fed daily by the spiritual bread of the Eucharist.

At another time in history, "daily bread" was understood to be the Word of God, often referred to in song, prose, and poetry as the bread of life. A familiar hymn, written by Mary Ann Lathbury in 1877, sings:

> Break Thou the bread of life, dear Lord to me,
> As Thou didst break the loaves beside the sea;
> Beyond the sacred page I seek Thee, Lord;
> My spirit pants for Thee, O living Word![59]

Asking God to give us our daily bread was asking God to give us a daily dose of truth and inspiration from the Bible.

At another time in history, the bread was said to be Jesus. Jesus called himself the Bread of Life in John's Gospel (John 6:33–35). Every day one was to receive Jesus into one's life, and to feast on his love and grace and forgiveness. Give us today our daily bread, the bread of life, who is Jesus the Christ.

Some took this in a purely Jewish sense to mean the bread of the heavenly kingdom. The Jews of Jesus' day had an apocalyptic belief that when the Messiah came sometime in the future, a golden age would emerge. They called this the Messianic Banquet, where the chosen of God would sit down with the Christ and share a meal. The butchered meat of the biblical monsters Behemoth and the sea monster Leviathan would be the entrées. The Messiah would preside at the table and those invited would be the chosen ones.[60] So when one prayed, "Give us today our daily bread," one would be asking God to make sure that one's name would be among the place cards at the final, Messianic banquet of the people of God.

These may sound like strange interpretations to us in the twenty-first century, but in Christian history each was accepted, for a time, as a correct understanding. Yet this phrase "give us today our daily bread" sounds so simple and straightforward.

Our catechism gives a great interpretation:

A. 55. [We pray this way] because all good things come from God. Even in our most ordinary needs, God cares for us completely.

How hard is this to understand? God cares for us completely! Who could mix it up? Why make it more complicated than it really is?

What makes this phrase harder than it looks is the word "daily" as it is commonly translated in the traditional Lord's Prayer. The extraordinary fact is that, until just a few decades ago, there was no other known occurrence of this particular Greek word in all of Greek literature. Ancient scholars, like third-century Origen of Alexandria, just assumed that Matthew invented the word. For two thousand years it was impossible to know *exactly* what it meant. It was a one-of-a-kind word. Then archaeologists found a shopping list. Getting ready for a morning visit to the neighborhood Food Lion of Judah grocery store, someone had taken out a papyrus shopping list and quill pen, dipped it in ink, and written: <u>For the coming day</u>, I'll need: bread, wine, cheese, salted fish.[61]

For only the second time in the history of the world (as far as scholars know!) the Greek word for "daily" was written out. A fragment of papyrus, a shopping list, had biblical scholars doing cartwheels. "For the coming day." So very simply, what Jesus wants us to pray is:

"Give me the things we need to eat for this coming day. Help me to get the things I've got on my shopping list when I go to the store this morning. Give me the things we need to eat when the kids come in from school. Give me the menu items I'll need to fix dinner tonight." This is a simple prayer that God will supply us with the things we need *for the coming day.*[62]

Did Jesus intend for us to pray the Lord's Prayer in the morning? It appears that it directs us to ask God to give us what we need *for the day ahead.* That may have been the original intention, but perhaps it is good that this particular aspect of the Jesus Prayer was not understood for centuries. The Lord's Prayer could easily have been pigeonholed as the church's designated morning prayer, but because it was translated in a more general fashion, it has become a prayer for all seasons and for any hour of the day or night. Thanks be to God for obscure New Testament words!

Can you imagine what Christianity would be like if the Lord's Prayer were only used as a morning prayer? What would your faith be like if you did not use the Lord's Prayer as much as you do? I am glad we did not know the exact meaning of "daily." Our lack of understanding opened up the way for the Lord's Prayer to become the church's primary prayer. I think the church would be very different without it.

With this in mind, I would like to explore the catechism's question **Why do we pray, "Give us today our daily bread"?** and its answer: **All good things come from God. Even in our most ordinary needs, God cares for us completely.**

First, the prayer helps us to realize that we have to live "one day at a time" and not worry too much about tomorrow. If you think about it, "one day at a time" is all we have to work with, isn't it? "This is the day that the LORD has made; let us rejoice and be glad in it" (Ps. 118:24). This affirmation does not say, "Tomorrow is the day the Lord has made." One day at a time is what we get.

I am sure Jesus thought about the Hebrews in the wilderness and God providing manna, a bread-like nutrient, each morning. With little food, the Hebrews scrambled to collect enough manna for the coming day. Any left over, any packed away for the next day, would go bad. "Just enough for the coming day," God said. "No more, no less."

Second, this prayer helps us to acknowledge that God is the giver of all life. After so many discoveries of science made over the centuries, it is still impossible for us to create a tiny seed. We can clone, radiate, and genetically manipulate seeds to resist disease or to produce a larger grain, but we still cannot create a tiny seed. That is God's area of expertise. God provides for even our most ordinary needs.

Third, it helps us to understand the basic fact that prayer and work go hand in hand. Can you imagine a minister on Sunday morning, setting up the church for the monthly celebration of the Lord's Supper, praying, "Lord, give us the bread that we'll need for the coming day," and just standing there waiting for it to fall from heaven? Like faith, prayer without works is dead. When we pray, "Give us today our daily bread," we are saying two things: that without God we can do nothing, and that without our cooperation, God can do nothing for us.

Fourth, this phrasing of the Lord's Prayer helps us to remember that the prayer is plural. "Give *us* today our daily bread." It is not about me. It is not about just you. It is about us.

We recently remembered Allen at a service here. A member of this congregation, Allen was a man with a big heart, offering himself to numerous civic groups and charities. He was a Rotarian, and their motto, "Service above self," fit him. When we think of the "us" in "give us today," it would be good to think of that motto, "Service above self."

This is a prayer that we can help God answer by sharing our blessings with others who have daily needs. When we pray, "Give us today our daily bread," God's still, small voice is whispering in our ear, "Help me do this."

Lord, give us what we need for the coming day so that we may help others who have needs we can fulfill. Amen.

49

The Jesus Prayer 8

Exodus 32:30–32; Luke 18:9–14

Moses said to the people, "You have made a mistake. But now I will go up to the Lord; perhaps I can make amends for your mistake." So Moses returned to the Lord and said, "Alas, the people have made a mistake. If you will forgive their mistake, great, but if not, then count me out of your favor" (Ex. 32:30–32, paraphr.).

Jesus told a story. Two Presbyterians went up to the church to pray; an elder and the church janitor. The elder prayed, "Thank you, God, that I am not like the common people or even that janitor who has dirt under his nails. I'm so good." But the janitor could not even bring himself to look up, saying, "Be merciful to me; I made a mistake."

Have you noticed the subtle revision I made to the two biblical stories? Neither of them sounds very important or meaningful if we are talking only about mistakes they made rather than sins they committed. But so often I hear people calling sins "mistakes." A mistake is wearing a navy sweater with a black dress. A mistake is picking up the wrong car keys. A mistake is calling your grandchild by the wrong name. A mistake is forgetting it is your Sunday to teach church school. A mistake is bringing home your math book when you have English homework. A mistake is dialing your office number when you intended to call home.

Some mistakes are bigger than others. Toronto police approached a man outside a restaurant. Boy, did they make a mistake! The suspect taken into custody was one-time middleweight boxer Rubin "Hurricane" Carter, who had spent almost twenty years in a New Jersey prison for a triple murder he did not commit. Sixty years old at the time of the Toronto incident, he worked as the executive director of the Association in Defense of the Wrongfully Convicted. It was a case of mistaken identity, and the Toronto police offered to pay for damage caused by the search of his car. Understandably he remains angry. The last time he had been told he was under arrest, he didn't see the light of day for twenty years. Mistakes are one thing; sin is another. Christians are to apologize for mistakes and to do what we can to correct them. Mistakes are limited to human consequences, and we deal with them in a horizontal fashion. "My mistake. Here, let me make that right. How can I help fix it?"

Christians deal with sin in much the same way, but it is not only a horizontal interaction. It is a vertical one as well. In fact, when we think about dealing with sin, we cannot help thinking about how Jesus dealt with it, on the cross. With sin, we have to try to make things right with others—horizontally—but this is not possible until we get things ✝ right with God—vertically. A cross.

Mel Gibson made a movie about the life of Jesus. He made it as realistic as possible, including dialogue in Latin and Aramaic, two now-dead languages that were spoken in Jesus' day. Gibson, one of the most popular and powerful men in Hollywood, talks about the power of the cross: "Christ paid the price for all our sins. The struggle between good and evil, and the overwhelming power of love go beyond race and culture. This film is about faith, hope, love, and forgiveness. These are things that the world could use more of, particularly in these turbulent times."[63] He comments about the easy Christianity of our day: "I think we have gotten used to seeing to pretty crucifixes on the wall and we forget what really happened. I mean, we know that Jesus was scourged, that he carried his cross, that he had nails put through his hands and feet, but we rarely think about what this means."[64]

Gibson admits that he has grown into his strong faith: "Growing up I didn't realize what was involved in this. I didn't realize how hard it was. The full horror of what Jesus suffered for our redemption didn't really strike me. Understanding what he went through, even on a human level, makes me feel not only compassion, but also a debt: I want to repay him for the enormity of his sacrifice."[65] Mel Gibson reminds us that we owe Jesus such a debt that, on human terms, it can never be paid back,

Our sin was dealt with on the cross, a cross that vertically lifts our eyes to God and horizontally makes us reach out to those we've hurt. The Jesus Prayer puts it this way: "Forgive us our debts as we forgive our debtors." The contemporary catechism puts it into modern English:

Q. 56–57. What do we ask when we pray, "Forgive us our sins as we forgive those who sin against us"?

A. 56–57. Telling God we are sorry, we ask God not to hold our sins against us, but to accept us again by grace. We are to forgive others, just as God has forgiven us.

What are we praying about when we pray this part of the Jesus Prayer? There are four parts to this request: We tell God we're sorry; we ask God not to hold our sins against us; we hope God shows us grace; we pray that we can pass that grace on to others.

First, we tell God we're sorry. This is not the kind of "sorry" heard when a child is forced to say "sorry" to his little brother for punching him in the back. Nothing fake can be in this "sorry." It has to be *real*. This kind of regret is called compunction. Compunction literally means "the pricking of the conscience." That sounds painful, doesn't it? Compunction involves repentance—changing one's mind and then fitting one's actions to that change. It is hard and it hurts! It is a bitter realization to find that one is wrong.

That is why so few people do repent. And that's why so many people choose to call "sin" a mistake. We think we can avoid the pain by avoiding the vertical dimension of making things right.

Caught gossiping, Theodore apologized, saying, "I'm sorry, I guess I shouldn't have said that in front of you." However, sin cannot be dealt with as though it were no more than a mistake. Turning to God and to the one whom we have hurt, we need to confess the sin, make apologies, ask forgiveness, and change the hurtful behavior.

Caught gossiping, Dana prayed that night and asked God to forgive her. She asked God to help her find a way to avoid her friend who always gossiped and asked for courage to talk to the man she hurt that day. The next day she went to him and said, "I'm so sorry I hurt you. I will not do that again. Can you find it in your heart to forgive me?"

Vertically and horizontally. This is how a Christian deals with sin.

Second, we ask that God not hold our sins against us. An old-fashioned term for this is "mercy." Experiencing mercy means not getting what we deserve. Saul—a.k.a. Paul—held his cohorts' coats so they could have an unobstructed shot at Stephen. Rock after rock flew. Rock after rock pummeled his body. Even when he had fallen down, the rocks still fell on him until he was dead. Saul's snickering friends dusted off their hands, reclaimed their coats, and said, "He didn't last long. Too bad the fun was short-lived."

While Paul was on his way to do it again in Damascus, the Risen Lord confronted him. Did he get what he deserved? No. Jesus made him an apostle to the Gentiles! Mercy is not getting what you deserve.

Third, we ask God to show us grace. If mercy is not getting what we deserve, grace is getting what we don't deserve. In this case, we are given love, forgiveness, and a new chance at life.

Fourth, we ask God to help us pass on the grace "as we forgive those who sin against us." This is a part of the horizontal work to which we are called. It is our chance to experience something of God's nature: forgiving others, showing mercy, and offering grace.

Grace to you, and peace. Amen.

50

The Jesus Prayer 9

Luke 4:1–2; 1 Corinthians 10:12–13

The place: Central Iraq. With a loaded nine-millimeter pistol strapped to his thigh and a green flak jacket pinched around his chest, a soldier sat in a metal folding chair and held a small *Soldier's Book of Worship* above his right shoulder. Another soldier standing in the sand behind him began to strum notes to a hymn on his acoustic guitar. He wore a flak jacket embellished with a black patch, with the words "Strike to Kill" below an image of a cobra wound around a skull. He intoned: "Blessed Assurance, Jesus is mine! O what a foretaste of glory divine! . . ."

Sunday services at an Army infantry battalion were under way. Soldiers held prayer books in one hand, M-16s in the other. They wore camouflaged uniforms, Kevlar helmets, and flak jackets weighed down with gas masks, ammo clips, and knives. And sitting sun-baked in the desert in the middle of a Muslim county, soldiers told stories about Jesus and God and peace and divine protection.

For many men and women, their prayer life has become one of the most important weapons they carry into battle. For some, that battle is against a regime in the ancient homeland of Father Abraham. For the rest of us, it is a spiritual battle against a subtler enemy who often fights using guerrilla tactics of stealth and infiltration.

All who pray "Lead us not into temptation, but deliver us from evil" share the fight against temptation and evil influences, and even the evil powers themselves. And like the men and women of that Army battalion, we ask for God's divine protection when and where we need it most. Our contemporary catechism asks:

Q. 58. What do we ask when we pray, "Save us from the time of trial, and deliver us from evil"?

A. 58. We ask God to protect us, especially when we most need it. We pray for God to free us from all desires that would lead us to sin, and to shelter us from the powers of evil that may threaten us.

The Jesus Prayer deals with two equally deadly threats to God's people: first, the power of temptation and its desires that lead us to sin; and second, the power of evil itself. By calling on God to help us avoid and overcome these two equally troubling threats, we admit that we need God's divine protection because there are some things we just cannot do on our own. In Psalm 146 we are told, "Don't put your trust in human leaders; no person can save you. Happy is the one who depends on the Lord" (Ps. 146:3, 5, paraphr.). When it comes to temptation and evil in the world, the Lord's Prayer directs us to the One who can indeed help—our Father in heaven.

Have you ever seen the bumper sticker that says, "I can resist anything but temptation"? Temptation is strong stuff. No wonder the Evil One uses it so much! It is a threat to all of us! As Christians, we know it takes maturity, will power, and often help from others to resist temptation, because we cannot always do it on our own. We need God's help.

Paul warned: "Whoever thinks you're standing firm had better be careful that you don't fall. Every test that you've experienced is the kind that normally comes to people. But God will keep his promises, God will not allow you to be tested beyond your power to remain firm, and God will give you the power to resist and offer a way out" (1 Cor. 10:12–13, paraphr.). When Jesus was tempted he found a way out. His defense was to go to God's Word. There he found promises he could count on to protect him when he was most vulnerable, in the wilderness. Pray that God will protect you from temptation. Hold on to the promise of God. Jesus says, pray this way: "Our Father, protect us, especially when we most need it, and free us from all desires that would lead us to sin."

"Deliver us from evil" is a four-worded request with no "ifs," "ands," or "buts." Jesus says, "Pray this way: . . . O Lord, deliver us from evil."

One Wednesday a Methodist pastor and I were planning the community Maundy Thursday Service. After we put away our scribbled notes and final outline, we talked about what each was going to preach about the following week. I told him that I was going to address the phrase in the Lord's Prayer "Deliver us from evil," and he told me that he was going to preach the message that we need to pray for God to deal with the evil in the world. It was one of those neat coincidences that got us both talking nonstop.

Carl, the pastor, said he was growing weary of just praying that God would protect us, especially since a number of our church members have been brought into harm's way by their military service. I agreed. Carl said that it was beginning to seem as though we are whining to God, and that God is so much more powerful than we will allow. I agreed. I said that the Lord's Prayer is blunt about it. No "ifs," "ands," or "buts," only a four-word statement: "Deliver us from evil." He agreed. "Can't we start praying for God not just to protect us alone, but also that God will rid our world of evil?" I agreed. Carl and I both said that we must start praying right now that God will deliver the entire world from evil. We both agreed.

So we will do that now:

Our Father, confront the evil in this world,
the evil that takes over the hearts of some of us;

the evil that allows some in authority to see rape, murder,
mutilation, torture, poisoning, oppression, and humiliation
as simply means to their ends.
Confront and defeat evil in the hearts of persons and in regimes
that are built on doctrines that transgress your Holy Name
and count people as cannon fodder.
Deliver the world from evil's long reach
and protect all people from its harm and fear.
As your people, keep us from evil acts and thoughts.
May we not return evil for evil, but return good for evil,
for the sake of your Son, who confronted evil on the cross
and won.
We are more than victors in Jesus' name. Amen.

51

The Jesus Prayer 10

1 Chronicles 29:11–12; Philippians 2:9–11; Matthew 11:1–10

For the kingdom, the power, and the glory are yours, now and forever." The Lord's Prayer has what we might call its own epilogue. It ends in threefold praise. In a little devotional book on the Lord's Prayer, William Barclay writes:

"For Thine is the kingdom . . ."

We end the prayer recognizing that God is King and that we are subjects. Then we pledge our obedience and our allegiance to God.[66]

"For Thine is the power . . ."

We end our prayer in the confidence that God has heard our prayer and that in God's dynamic power he will answer.[67]

"For Thine is the glory . . ."

We end the prayer by reminding ourselves that we are in the presence of the divine glory; and that means that we must live life within the splendor of the glory of God.[68]

The contemporary catechism, *Belonging to God*, asks,

Q. 59. What does it mean to pray, "For the kingdom, the power, and the glory are yours now and forever"?

A. 59. We praise God for being able and willing to do everything we have asked in this prayer. We give ourselves over to God's wise and gracious rule, and we know that God can be trusted to make all things work together for good, now and forever.

We conclude the Lord's Prayer with praise—praise that the Lord is King, powerful and worthy of glory; praise, like spontaneous combustion, erupted from pilgrims hiking up the hard-packed road to the gates of Jerusalem. They saw Jesus and shouted out, "King! Power! Glory!"—an accolade to his many sermons and his amazing miracles. Yet, as Barclay says, "the whole picture is of a populace who misunderstood."[69] Jesus was revealing a brand new meaning to these words.

In the Gospel text, Jesus appears not to protest the parade. He seems to encourage the event. "Sing on. Sing on and join the parade!" we can hear him say. The disciples move with Jesus, keeping Jesus at their shoulders and within easy reach. There are reports, the kind you take seriously, that there is a contract out on him. They stay close by. But do the people really know what it means to praise him as king, powerful and glorious? He is entering the holy city, but why? Is it a march to overthrow the government? Is it a peasants' revolt? Is it laity against clergy? Jews against Romans? Jesus against the establishment? Is it just a fun parade? Everybody loves a parade! What might Jesus say to these hasty volunteers? Perhaps he would ask, **"Are you sure you wish to follow me?"**

Three years before, the same question was raised. Andrew, Peter, Matthew, John, James, and the rest answered, "Yes, Lord. We will follow you." Now, the same question had an edge to it. "Are you sure you are willing to pay the price? It will cost you more than you can imagine."

One pilgrim made her way to Jesus. Her cloak was woven of fine Arabian linen. She waved it and sang, "King! Power! Glory!" She said to him, "We're so glad you've come. We need you so badly in our city. Tell me if you've come to answer my prayers."

She handed Jesus a slip of paper on which was written a prayer in the form of a poem. Obviously from the condition of the parchment, she must have been praying this prayer every day for a long, long time. The prayer read as follows: "On the streets I saw a small girl, cold and shivering in a thin dress, with little hope of a decent meal. I became angry and said to God: 'Why don't you do something about it?' "

Jesus reread the prayer aloud this time. "Why don't *you* do something about it?" he said.

The woman said, "Yes! Why don't you do something about it?"

Jesus read it aloud again, "Why don't *you* do something about it?"

"Yes," she said. "Why don't you do something about it?"

Jesus said, "You're not getting it."

"Getting what?"

"Getting it! God did do something about it. God created *you!* Why don't *you* do something about it? Are you sure you want to follow me?"

She took her cloak and wrapped it around her shoulders and walked away from the parade.

Jesus said, "In my parade, when you see someone cold and shivering, and give her a cloak, it is as if you are doing it for me."

Two men joined the parade as it neared the walls of Jerusalem. They marched with Jesus, praising him—"King, power and glory!" Broad smiles arched across their faces and they picked up palm branches, waving them and shouting. They nudged closer to Jesus, pushing aside an older woman, forcing children out of the way. Jesus stepped in front of a child with a crutch, and he turned, pulling the child to his side. Jesus lifted the young boy onto the donkey's back with him. Insulted, the two men complained, "Messiah, we've come to join your cause and this is how you treat us?"

Jesus said, "In my parade there are no distinctions between men or women, rich or poor, slave or free citizen, Jew or Gentile. Whoever doesn't take up their cross and follow me isn't fit to join the parade. Whoever tries to push to the head of the line will be sent back, but whoever gives their place in line to another will come to the front. Do you still want to follow me?"

The two men dropped their palm branches and let the procession go by.

Into the parade came a clergyman. His robes announced his holy calling and all eyes turned and watched as he made his way to Jesus. He listened as the people shouted, "King! Power! Glory!" His head said to leave this rabble as quick as possible, but his heart said to stay. "King! Power! Glory!" resonated in the chambers of his curious heart. Brushing up against the crowds, the clergyman bumped into a village woman who was missing her wedding headdress, the chain with coins hanging from it like charms. No respectable Jewish woman would be seen in public without it. She must have been divorced or, worse, she might be a woman of ill repute. Jewish law made it clear that touching her, even brushing up against her dress, would make the clergyman ritually unclean. He would not be able to enter the Temple in that state of spiritual disorder. He would be defiled. That is when he heard Jesus say to her, "Neither do I condemn you. Go in peace and sin no more. Are you sure want to follow me?"

She said, "I will follow you."

The genuineness of the moment so overwhelmed the clergyman's sense of order that he moved closer to Jesus in spite of the pressing crowds. Jesus turned to the priest, and said, "Just as salt can lose its savor, so can an initial commitment, however sincere. It can fade over the course of time. Are you sure you want to follow me?"

For the moment, the clergyman continued along in the parade. Jesus put his arm around the clergyman's shoulder and said, "Under pressures both open and subtle, pressures we all know, salt doesn't decide to be pepper; it just gradually loses its savor. The process can be so gradual, in fact, that no one really notices . . . well, almost no one."

The parade entered the Temple courtyard to the shouts of "King! Power! Glory!" and we echo those shouts today. Jesus says to us in the church, "Are you sure you want to follow me?" If so, then take up your cross, open your heart, extend a helping hand, expand your horizons, and join the parade!

It is time for us to shout, "Praise to you, King, Power, and Glory!" Amen.

52

Amen and Amen

2 Corinthians 1:20; Mark 16:1-7

Amen is an Easter word! Our contemporary catechism, *Belonging to God*, asks in its final question:

Q. 60. Why does our prayer end with "Amen"?

A. 60. "Amen" means "so be it" or "let it be so." It expresses our complete confidence in God, who makes no promise that will not be kept and whose love endures forever.

Amen and Easter go together as naturally as a rainbow follows a storm or a butterfly comes from a caterpillar. Easter is the Amen to the cross. The empty tomb on Sunday validated what Jesus did on Friday. When we say "Easter," we are saying "Amen!" Amen means "So be it!" It is the little word that means that God is going to do what God promises to do. Amen means "Yes, it's true!" Easter is the Amen to the cross.

Amen is a Hebrew word that has been passed down through the New Testament Greek language and into English without much change. In Hebrew, the word is pronounced "ah main." In the Greek of the New Testament it sounds much the same. In English, it is often given one "a" sound (like the letter a) when spoken and another "a" sound (ah) when sung.[70]

In Hebrew, *amen* means "firm" or "reliable." In Greek, it means "truly" or "surely." In English it means "true" or "Yes, it is true." According to its many uses in the Bible, *amen* can be a stamp of approval (Jer. 28:6) or a "me too" at the close of a prayer (Rev. 5:13). In Old Testament days, an *amen* could confirm a contract between two parties (Num. 5:22), and it is another way of saying, "Thus says the Lord." Jesus said it often: "Surely, surely (or Amen, amen), I say to you" (see especially the Gospel of John).

In Paul's day it was expected that everyone in church would say "amen" at the end of a prayer (Rev. 5:13). In David's day, it was the way the Israelites affirmed the Tabernacle prayers and psalms. When Jesus went to synagogue, the congregation would answer "ah main" (*amen*) at the end of the prescribed prayers. The synagogue in Alexandria, Egypt, was so large that often the crowd could not hear the prayers and a flag was waved to signal the congregation when to say *amen*.[71] Wouldn't that be something to see! And in Revelation 3:14, Jesus is called "AMEN" because he is a factual witness—nothing besides truth is in him. He is the Great AMEN—"yes, it is true!"

In other words, Easter is God's great Amen. The empty tomb on Sunday validated what Jesus did on Friday. Easter is the Amen! ("Yes! It is true!") when the world asks, "Did Jesus save the world from sin by his death on the cross?" The empty tomb is God's "Amen!" or God's "Yes!"

Without the Amen! of Easter, the world would still be wondering if the cross were a tool for grace or just Jesus' last known address. Without the Amen! of Easter, the church would have a question mark (?) as its symbol instead of an empty cross. Without the Amen! of Easter, we would still be wondering about life beyond death. The Amen! of Easter says, "It is true!"

In our day, declaring something to be true does not necessarily make it so. The television screen is split in two as we watch the news. There are different takes on events around on the world and contradicting reports about the war in Iraq. When the Jewish authorities found out that the tomb was empty and Jesus' body was missing, they concocted a story that someone stole the body and carried it away. They paid off the guards and spread the false story: "Of course the tomb is empty; someone stole the corpse and hid it."

On July 15, 1997, Barney the purple dinosaur caught on fire. The cooling unit in the sixty-pound costume short-circuited and smoke filled the insides, sending the actor to the hospital. The story of the incident was reported on the news that night and parents called the show by the hundreds, saying their children were afraid Barney had been burned, or worse, that he was a fake. A fake! For a three-year-old, that is a devastating revelation. Having one's fantasy crushed hurts. Childhood fantasies like Barney can bring children good feelings. But when adults pretend a lie is the truth, reality becomes distorted. Sooner or later, fantasies break down and the truth comes out. Yes, it is true that dinosaurs cannot dance and sing. And yes, it is true that the empty tomb validates everything about Jesus' life. Easter is God's Amen!

For those who may be wondering, "Will my sins be forgiven?" God says, "Amen! Your sins are forgiven!"

For those who may be wondering, "What happens after death?" God says, "Amen! Heaven awaits you on the other side!"

For those who may be wondering if God loves them, God says, "Amen! I love you so much I died for you!"

For those who may be wondering if God is still interested in their lives, God says, "Amen, my beloved! The persons you are today are what I created you for. You are my Easter people!"

I'm a big David Bailey fan. David is a singer-songwriter whose songs are filled with the grace of God. He is a cancer survivor and the son of a Presbyterian missionary family. David played a concert for our church a few years ago, and he has made several CDs. My wife, Debbie, and I were listening to one of them in the car recently, and his closing song reminded me of how God says, "Amen! You are my Easter people!"

David introduces the closing song, "One More Day," with the truth that when today is over, it will be gone forever. We will never be able to get it back. He says that every time he gives a concert, he always wonders if maybe his entire life was all about getting him ready and giving him experience so that he could be right were he was that night, and that maybe that will be it. Maybe after that night his purpose on earth would be finished.

I have a friend who likes playing golf. He says he likes this sport because no matter how he plays one hole, he gets to start all over again on the next one. It's life! No matter what happens today, God willing, you get a chance to start all over tomorrow. And most of us don't even remember asking for one more day. And if we wake up tomorrow, it means there's something else we're supposed to do and that God still believes in us.

There's no guarantee that I'm going to wake up, or you either; but if you do, then it is true that God has given you a dream that's still rumbling around in your heart. It's true that God's given you "one more day."[72]

God said, "Amen!" to your life when you woke up this morning, and it well may be that your entire life was all about getting you ready and giving you experiences so you could be right where you are in the present moment. Maybe God has given you one more day to find out you are one of God's Easter people and God is saying, "Amen!" to your life right now.

If you wake up tomorrow, it means that God has given you one more day, and to that, again, God says, "Amen and amen!"

Notes

1. Heidelberg Catechism (1563), *Book of Confessions* (Louisville: Office of the General Assembly, Presbyterian Church [U.S.A.], 1999), 4.001.
2. Westminster Shorter Catechism, *Book of Confessions*, 7.001.
3. Confession of 1967, *Book of Confessions*, 9.17.
4. Westminster Shorter Catechism, *Book of Confessions*, 7.001.
5. M. Craig Barnes, *Hustling God* (Grand Rapids: Zondervan Publishing House, 1999), 24.
6. Ibid.
7. Frederick Buechner, *Wishful Thinking: A Theological ABC* (New York: Harper & Row, 1973), 34.
8. Curt Cloninger, *God Views: Seeing Clearly the One Who Loves You Most*, LifeSprings Resources, 2001, *www.curtcloninger.com*. Used with permission.
9. Patrick D. Miller, *Deuteronomy*, Interpretation: A Bible Commentary for Teaching and Preaching, ed. James Luther Mays (Louisville: John Knox Press, 1990), 103.
10. From Alice Gray and Barbara Baumgardner, eds., *Stories for a Kindred Heart* (Portland, OR: Multnomah Publishers, 2000), 280.
11. Jimmy Carter, *Sources of Strength: Meditations on Scripture for a Living Faith* (New York: Times Books, 1997), 142–43.
12. Carl Sagan, *Contact* (New York: Pocket Books, 1985).
13. Craig Larson, *Choice Contemporary Stories & Illustrations* (Grand Rapids: Baker Books, 1998), 55.
14. Tony Campolo, *How to Rescue the Earth without Worshiping Nature* (Nashville: Thomas Nelson, 1992), video.
15. Larson, *Choice Contemporary Stories & Illustrations*, 154.
16. Donald G. Barnhouse, *Let Me Illustrate* (Westwood, NJ: Revell, 1967), 132.
17. James Montgomery Boice, *Foundations of the Christian Faith: A Comprehensive and Readable Theology*, rev. ed. (Downers Grove, IL: InterVarsity Press, 1986), 153.
18. Geoffrey Wainwright, *Doxology: The Praise of God in Worship, Doctrine and Life: A Systematic Theology* (New York: Oxford University Press, 1980), 30.
19. David Bailey, "Trying to Believe," 2005. Used with permission.
20. Romans 7:15–24; Eugene H. Peterson, *The Message: The New Testament in Contemporary Language* (Colorado Springs, CO: Navpress, 1993), 2047.
21. Max Lucado, *In the Eye of the Storm: A Day in the Life of Jesus* (W Publishing Group, 2002), 105–106.
22. Annie Dillard, *Pilgrim at Tinker Creek* (New York: Harper & Row, 1974), 5–6.
23. C. S. Lewis, *Mere Christianity* (New York: Macmillian, 1943), 106.
24. Rudy Giuliani, Commencement Address, Syracuse University, Syracuse, New York, May 12, 2002.
25. Larson, *Choice Contemporary Stories & Illustrations*, 92.
26. William R. White, *Stories for the Journey* (Minneapolis: Augsburg, 1988), 91.
27. Kathleen Norris, *Amazing Grace: A Vocabulary of Faith* (New York: Riverhead Books, 1998), 161.
28. Sid Fleischman, *The Whipping Boy* (Mahwah, NJ: Troll Books, 1986), 1–4.
29. Buechner, *Wishful Thinking*, 83–84.
30. Steve May, *The Story File: 1,001 Contemporary Illustrations for Speakers, Writers & Preachers* (Peabody, MA: Steve May, 2000), 286.
31. This story was told by Nicky Gumbel at an Alpha Course presentation.
32. C. S. Lewis, *The Lion, the Witch and the Wardrobe: A Story for Children* (New York: Collier Books, 1950).
33. John Bartlett and Justin Kaplan, eds., *Familiar Quotations* (Boston: Little, Brown, 1992), 684:19.
34. William H. Willimon, *Acts*, Interpretation: A Bible Commentary for Teaching and Preaching, ed. James Luther Mays (Atlanta: John Knox Press, 1988), 22.
35. I. Howard Marshall, *Acts*, Tyndale New Testament Commentaries (Downers Grove, IL: InterVarsity Press, 1980), 59–60.

36. Office of Theology and Worship, "Hope in the Lord Jesus Christ" (Louisville: Presbyterian Church [U.S.A.], 2002), lines 195–200.

37. Only males were present.

38. *The Interpreter's Dictionary of the Bible*, ed. George A. Buttrick (Nashville: Abingdon Press, 1962), 2:446.

39. Jack Haberer, guest editorial, *Presbyterian Outlook Online*, October 14, 2002, p. 4, *www.pres-outlook.com/haberer101402.html.*

40. Ephesians 3:14–21; Peterson, *The Message,* 407.

41. Heidelberg Catechism (1563), *Book of Confessions* (Louisville: Office of the General Assembly, Presbyterian Church [U.S.A.], 2002), Q. 1.

42. David L. Mueller, *Karl Barth,* Makers of the Modern Theological Mind (Waco, TX: Word Books, 1972), 37–38.

43. William Gentz, ed., *The Dictionary of Bible and Religion* (Nashville: Abingdon Press, 1986), 914.

44. Loyal Jones, ed., *The Preacher Joke Book* (Little Rock: August House, 1989), 77–79.

45. "Great Is Thy Faithfulness," *The Presbyterian Hymnal* (Louisville: Westminster/John Knox Press, 1990), no. 276.

46. Ibid.

47. The Joint Office of Worship for the Presbyterian Church (U.S.A.) and the Cumberland Presbyterian Church, *The Service for the Lord's Day,* Supplemental Liturgical Resource 1 (Philadelphia: Westminster Press, 1984), 16.

48. Edward Chinn, *The Wonder of Words: One Hundred Words and Phrases Shaping How Christians Think and Live* (Lima, OH: C.S.S. Publishing Co., 1985), 7.

49. YHWH is known as the Tetragrammaton in biblical studies.

50. John Calvin, *Institutes of the Christian Religion,* 1.13.1; ed. John T. McNeill, trans. Ford Lewis Battles (Philadelphia: Westminster Press, 1960), 1:120–21.

51. John Gibson, *Genesis,* vol. 1, The Daily Study Bible (Philadelphia: Westminster Press, 1981), 19–20.

52. John Macquarrie, *Principles of Christian Theology,* 2nd ed. (New York: Charles Scribner's Sons, 1977), 203–204.

53. William Barclay, *The Gospel of Matthew,* Daily Study Bible—New Testament, vol. 1 (Philadelphia: Westminster Press, 1975), 204.

54. Ibid., p. 205.

55. Clarence Jordan, *Sermon on the Mount* (Valley Forge, PA: Judson Press, 1952), 87.

56. Barclay, *Matthew,* 205.

57. Emil Brunner, quoted in "God, Names of," *International Standard Bible Encyclopedia,* vol. 2, ed. Geoffrey W. Bromiley (Grand Rapids: Eerdmans, 1982), 504.

58. Ecclesiastes 3:1–8, New International Version (International Bible Society, 1984).

59. Mary Ann Lathbury, "Break Thou the Bread of Life," *The Presbyterian Hymnal* (Louisville: Westminster/John Knox Press. 1990), no. 329.

60. Barclay, *Matthew,* 216.

61. Ibid., 217.

62. Ibid.

63. "Mel Gibson's Great Passion: Christ's Agony as You've Never Seen It," Zenit News Services, March 6, 2003, *www.zenit.org.*

64. Ibid.

65. Ibid.

66. William Barclay, *The Lord's Prayer: Pocket Guide* (1973; Louisville: Westminster John Knox Press, 2001), 64.

67. Ibid.

68. Ibid.

69. William Barclay, *The Gospel of Mark,* Daily Study Bible—New Testament (Philadelphia: Westminster Press, 1975), 266.

70. *The International Standard Bible Encyclopedia,* vol. 1, ed. Geoffrey W. Bromiley (Grand Rapids: Eerdmans, 1979), 110.

71. *Interpreter's Dictionary of the Bible,* 1:105.

72. "Live," by David M. Bailey, 2001. Used with permission.